Monsieur Geo Nicholson
Curator, Royal Gardens
Kew.

Monsieur T. ...
à Ch...

Cher Monsieur,

Votre lettre datée du 21 juillet ne m'est parvenue que vers le 15 7bre par suite de la méprise qui lui avait fait prendre une fausse direction. La saison est donc trop avancée maintenant pour vous expédier ... odorata exquisita ... sulfurea ... ... helvola ... Kewi rosea ... doit être renvoyé au ... prochain et je vous ... plantes à cette époque ... aux lettres, à moins ... ne me donniez un avis ...

... mon respectueux dévouement.

B. Latour Marliac

Cher Monsieur

... Richardson ... Nymphæa ...

Miss Jekyll — Godalming
11 mai   4
6 mai
£ 0-17-6

B. Latour Marliac

10 mai, en un colis postal marqué du N° 3.

5 Nymphæa Marliacea rosea à 4^f	20	
Port et emballage	2	10
Total	22	10

Soit en monnaie anglaise £ 0-17-6
Nous n'avons pu fournir que 5 Water
Lilies ... de cette espèce

WATER LILIES

and BORY LATOUR-MARLIAC,
the genius behind Monet's Water Lilies

WATER LILIES

and BORY LATOUR-MARLIAC,
the genius behind Monet's Water Lilies

Caroline Holmes
Photographs by Peter Evans

GARDEN • ART • PRESS

ISBN 978 1 87067 383 9

Frontispiece: A statue of Joseph Bory Latour-Marliac cradling a water lily in his hand with
one of the fourteen springs behind him. The sculptor is Lloyd Le Blanc.

Title page: Rothschild Head Gardener James Hudson was one of Latour-Marliac's key
English customers. After Latour-Marliac's death, his son Édgard commemorated their
friendship in 1912 with the *Nymphaea* 'James Hudson'.

Printed in China
for the Garden Art Press, an imprint of ACC Art Books Ltd.,
Woodbridge, Suffolk IP12 4SD

Victoria **'Longwood Hybrid'.** Hector the French bulldog demonstrates the strength of the leaves.

Contents

Preface

When researching Monet's gardens and plants I discovered that the original nursery where he had bought his water lilies still existed. I made contact and was duly invited. Throughout this book references are made to invitations exhorting friends and professionals to visit their water gardens in summer with the sun high in the sky and certainly no later than 5pm. Research constraints meant I made my first visit to the Latour-Marliac source in February 2001, the nursery lay bare-boned and bleak but the welcome was warm. I was entranced by the unbroken link, the sinuous shapes of the dish lined pools, the workaday rectangular ponds and the flowering rosemary that lined the path down to the lake.

Monet needs no introduction but the genesis of his greatest motif – the water lily – is the extraordinary enterprise of my hero Joseph Bory Latour-Marliac. While Monet painted second by second as the light changed, with equal artistry Latour-Marliac painstakingly mixed and matched his water lily palette. The results of Latour-Marliac's labours can grace any reader's piece of water – the same cannot be said for a Monet canvas.

For me one of the best aspects of my work is to handle the same documents as the person I am researching, the ebb and flow of their handwriting draws you into their personality. In what I later learnt was Édgard Latour-Marliac's villa, then home to Barbara and Ray Davies, I was shown thirty-four bound volumes of hand-written orders and letters addressed to many of my gardening heroes juxtaposed with routine orders and loving exchanges with family. I made feverish notes and vowed that at some point I would return to research further.

A small part of Monet's *Les Grandes Décorations* which line the walls of Musée de l'Orangerie in Paris.

The trail went cold until August 2009 when staying with friends in La Bastide-d'Armagnac I decided to take a not too distant pilgrimage back. Accompanied by my husband, David, we entered through the newly built boutique, he spotted a French edition of my book, *Monet at Giverny*. I approached the young man on the desk to introduce myself as the happy author. As we chatted in French I tried to work out his accent – Parisian seemed the most likely – until finally asking his name: Robert Sheldon came the reply, I riposted well that's not a French name, unsurprising as he is American. Why don't we speak English? We did.

I learnt that the archives were still on site awaiting research, we were both equally enthusiastic that their contents should be fully surveyed. Firstly, I wrote an article for *The Garden* magazine published in January 2011 to mark the centenary of

Latour-Marliac's death. Simultaneously we were in final negotiations with Garden Art Press for this book. There followed three years of visits, eye aching but fascinating, balanced by walking the surrounding countryside gaining a sense of place. In the tradition of Bory Latour-Marliac, Robert Sheldon is also a great host, excellent cook and cocktail maker so I was sustained throughout. My quarters were interesting, either in the very sparsely furnished Édgard's villa or alongside the prune oven with an array of spiders. I witnessed the changing seasons, the damp chill of winter, warmth of spring and the heat of several summers. I also weeded the lake, listened to the frogs and saw my first red squirrel kittens. Finally the joy of reading Bory's words to his son in Indochina 'Farewell my dear Édgard, I embrace you from the bottom of my heart with a tenderness as great as the distance that separates us'.

Nymphs and lotus eaters – the romance of Water Lilies

'It is not only from the mountain's breast dyed with Violet and Gentian, the Sunflower-strewn prairie of the north, or the sunny fields where Proserpine gathered flowers, that our garden flora comes. River and stream are often fringed with handsome plants, and little fleets of Water-Lily - silvery fleets they look as one sees them from the bank - sail on the lakelets far away in North America and Asia.'

William Robinson *The English Flower Garden* 1883

The Lotus

The word nymph evokes visions of an ethereal sprite, a will o'the wisp hovering over the water surface, divine spirits that animate nature. The nymphs that populated the calm springs and rivers of myth and legend were known as 'naiads' or 'limniads'; surely it is their spirits that inhabit the water lily genus, *Nymphaea*. The Lotus, or *Nelumbo* species, with their fragrant and exquisite chalice-shaped flowers, has also been described as a water lily. The difference lies in their hearts – the Lotus rapidly produces an architectural centrepiece like an elegant watering can rose, whereas the stamens at the centre of water lilies curl like bright saffron threads.

The synonyms for the European White Pond Lily illustrate its fragrance and poetics – 'Sweet Water Lily', 'Sweet-scented Water Lily', 'Water Nymph', and 'Large White Water Lily'. In *The Englishman's Flora* Geoffrey Grigson records further regional variations such as 'Lady of the Lake' in Cheshire and 'Swan among the Flowers' in Dorset and Wiltshire. The latter echoed in the Latour-Marliac *Nymphaea* 'Lac des Cygnes' named and commercialised by Robert Sheldon in 2009 from an unnamed 1992 variety. Grigson also recorded delightful regional substitute names such as 'Bobbins' in Scotland and 'Queen of the River' or 'Water Cups' in Somerset.

Lotuses are native to Eastern North America, across warm Asia to Australia, and their seeds can survive in the mud for several hundred years. They have long been grown in and around the Mediterranean so may well have been introduced by Roman spice traders. In Book IX of Homer's *The Odyssey*, Odysseus describes how, after nine days wracked by tumultuous seas, he and his men reached the land of the lotus-eaters. Once they had eaten the honeysweet fruit, their desire to travel home deserted them so he had to drag them, weeping, back to the ship to voyage onwards. Legend of equally mythical proportions surrounds the identification of this wonder-fruit. It could be the sacred lotus, *Nelumbo nucifera*, or the more highly scented and lightly psychedelic, Sacred Blue Lotus, *Nymphaea caerulea*, or the luscious fruits of the jujube tree, *Zizyphus jujuba*, whose botanical name is derived from the Arabic word used for the lotus fruit – *zizouf*. Tennyson's sybaritic Lotos-Eaters lived on jujube.

Above: *Nymphaea* 'Gonnère' (1914, Latour-Marliac). Named for Bory Latour-Marliac's wife Alida.

Facing page: *Nymphaea* 'Escarboucle'. The radiant crimson of the flower clearly reflected in the water which also mirrors the roses growing on the nearby pergola. A light confetti of white blossom enhances the effect.

Facing page: The pink lotus pool at Latour-Marliac. During the summer, several of Latour-Marliac's original pools featured lotuses, *Nelumbo* 'Osiris', which continues today and can be seen here rising sentinel from the abundance of their leaves. The Lotus is taken as a symbol of female beauty in China, whereas in Japan it is an emblem of purity.

Left: *Nelumbo nucifera.* An airborne bee prepares to alight onto a pink lotus, *Nelumbium.*

'It is this plant that is the Sphinx's coiffure, the lingerie of Isis, the throne of Harpocrates, the emblem of silence and perfection, it is the date of the Indes, carrying Brahma on the precipice to the eternal waters, or serving as a floating conch for the divine Lakchmi'.

A.L.A. Fée, 1822, *Flore deVirgile ou Catalogue Raisonné des plantes citées dans ses ouvrages*

Overleaf: *Nelumbo.* Although classed as tender, Robert Sheldon believes this to be simplistic. Lotus are hardy in areas which enjoy a constantly hot summer followed by a cold winter. Thus nourished by the sun they can hibernate successfully in the pond mud.

In Buddhism, the heart of the *Nelumbo nucifera* represents a host of human souls held fast in life whilst they attempt divine contemplation; once they are considered ready they are taken into the sacred presence. In other words, the core of the lotus is a microcosm of the world as a transient reflection of Buddha. The strength of the stems is such that the flowers continue to rise above the water, which is interpreted as representing the progress of the soul from cloying darkness through the waters of experience into enlightenment. There are countless depictions of Buddha seated on a lotus flower or standing with each foot on separate flowers. It is used as a decorative motif in Buddhist architecture, ceramics and textiles. The lotus (mental and spiritual purity) is one of Buddhism's Eight Auspicious Symbols, another is 'Golden Fishes' (happiness, fertility and salvation), which marries well with the creation of a lotus pool. In the ancient Sri Lankan city of Polonnaruwa, a 'Lotus Pond' survives from the Jetavana Monastery. Eight tiers representing the layers of petals that finally form the edges around which monks would have sat.

The Rev Hilderic Friend published *Flowers and Flower Lore* in 1886, recording that the *Nymphaea* was used on the Rhine as a charm against witchcraft. Two herbal authorities, Mrs M. Grieve and Mrs C.F. Leyel were English contemporaries of Édgard Latour-Marliac. The latter founded The Herb Society in 1927 and edited Grieve's life's work *A Modern Herbal* in 1931. Grieve describes the medicinal action of this 'aquatic herb':

'the roots could be used in [treating] dysentery, diarrhoea, gonorrhoea, and leucorrhoea as they are astringent, demulcent, anodyne, and anti-scrofulous. An infusion of the roots and leaves could be applied as a poultice to boils, tumours, scrofulous ulcers and inflamed skin. Alternatively you could gargle with an infusion for mouth and throat ulcers'.

Leyel published a host of herbal related books in which she includes Botanical, Country, French, German, Dutch, Italian, and Turkish names. In the case of the lotus she adds its name in Arabian, Indian, Malayan, Chinese and Persian.

Leyel writes of the heady perfumes and bright colours of Oriental water lilies whose roots can be roasted and eaten like potatoes whilst the seeds can be roasted or eaten raw like millet. For the controlling of pain she advised, in a similar vein to Grieve, making the leaves and roots of the hardy water lily into poultices to relieve the pain of boils, tumours and wounds of all kinds. She agrees with Grieve that the plants have a marked action on the organs of procreation.

The nocturnal, lightly fragrant white lotus of the Nile, *Nymphaea lotus* was noted in ∠60BC by Herodotus in his report on Egypt: 'When the Nile is full and has made the plains like a sea, great numbers of lilies spring up in the water; these they gather and dry in the sun, then having pounded the middle of the lotus, which resembles a poppy, they make bread of it and bake it. The root also of this lotus is fit for food, and is tolerably sweet, and is round and the size of an apple'. The origin of the biblical saying in Ecclesiastes 'Cast thy bread upon the waters, for thou shalt find it after many days' is said to come from the practice of pressing lotus seeds into balls of mud or clay mixed with chaff, which were then thrown out over water where they sank, hopefully to germinate.

As the pure white or pink flowers of the true sacred lotus arise from mud their symbolism is an association with sexual purity and non-attachment. In contrast the sprightly jaunts of

the classical world's nymphs are embedded in the words nympholepsy and nymphomania, a state of rapture inspired in men by nymphs and uncontrollable sexual desire in women. The water lily's sensuality oozes from the last verse of Tennyson's 'Now sleeps the Crimson Petal':

> Now folds the lily all her sweetness up,
> And slips into the bosom of the lake:
> So fold thyself, my dearest, thou, and slip
> Into my bosom and be lost in me.

In November 1986 the Mother (Baha'i) Temple of the Indian subcontinent was inaugurated in the village of Bahapur, which lies within the National Capital Territory of Delhi. The design was based on the opening flowers of the lotus to form a structure that creates a symbolic welcome to all denominations. A series of reflecting pools shaped like the flower's floating leaves frame this Lotus Temple, which is set in 26 acres. The structure is formed from three clusters of nine free-standing white marble-clad petals: the first two clusters of 18 petals curve inwards to embrace the inner dome; the third cluster curves outwards to form entrance canopies for each door on the nine sides. The Temple, in a design by Fariborz Sahba, a Canadian of Iranian origin, effectively holds the world in its petals.

The UK-based Institution of Structural Engineers presented the Temple with an award for excellence in religious art and architecture, citing:

> 'a building so emulating the beauty of a flower and so striking in its visual impact …

A Baha'i pilgrim wrote: 'May the fragrance of love and unity emanating from this heavenly 'Lotus of Bahapur' perfume the hearts and souls of diverse people and bind them together in praise of their Creator'. This spiritual sentiment curiously echoes the writings of our hero, the staunchly Catholic Joseph Bory Latour-Marliac.

Facing page: *Nelumbo* 'Osiris'. The Pink Lotus (Sanskrit *padma;* Tibetan *pad ma dmar po)* is the supreme lotus associated with the Great Buddha and generally reserved for the highest deity only. It is also Vietnam's national flower. Red Lotus (Sanskrit *kamala;* Tibetan *pad ma chu skyes)* signifies the original nature and purity of the heart (*hdrya)* and the qualities of love, compassion and passion. Blue Lotus (Sanskrit *utpala;* Tibetan *ut pa la)* symbolises the victory of the spirit over the senses, signifying the wisdom of knowledge.

Right: *Nelumbo* 'Alba Grandiflora'. The white Lotus (Sanskrit *pundarika;* Tibetan *pad ma dkar po)* represents the state of spiritual perfection and mental purity (*bodhi).*

Nelumbo nucifera. The Lotus flowers form a seed head that looks like a watering can rose. All parts of the *N. nucifera* are used in Chinese medicine: leaves (*he ye)*, leaf stalk (*lian geng)*, flower stalk with receptacle attached (*lian fang)*, rhizomes (*ou jie)*, flower stamens (*lian zu)*, seeds (*lian zi)* and, lastly, the seed plumule and radicle (*lian zi xin).*

The Mediterranean Sea throbbed at the heart of the classical world across which powerful gods such as Poseidon ruled, the almighty power of the sea meeting the steady flow of the River Gods from their source. That great symbol of virtue overcoming vice, Hercules, who can be seen resting after his labours in many great European gardens, is said to be the genesis of the water lily. Legend recounts that a maiden drowned herself for love of Hercules and was metamorphosed into a floating flower that blooms at the gates of Paradise.

The wide, navigable River Garonne with her handmaiden the River Lot flowing towards Bordeaux provided a vital source for the work of Joseph Bory Latour-Marliac. Colour and exuberance in tropical water lilies set him on the quest to bring such beauty to the temperate pools of France and beyond.

Above: The springs and lake in the Latour-Marliac grounds drain into the River Lot south of the village of Le Temple-sur-Lot. The département of the Lot-et-Garonne derives its name from the River Lot, which rises in the Cévennes, and the larger Garonne, their confluence is near Aiguillon, as one they flow majestically on until debouching at Bordeaux.

Proudly describing himself as a Templais, M Alfiéri Dall'Agata, a 90-year-old resident of Le Temple-sur-Lot, whose father had come to work in the village in the Twenties, described swimming in the Lot as a boy and finding himself one day in the midst of a teeming brood of fresh water jellyfish, something never seen before or since. Their presence was attributed at the time to the water lily nursery. They were said to have arrived as stowaways in a shipment of exotic water lilies from Zanzibar or another far-flung place and had found their way into the Lot via the stream, *Ruisseau de la Grésille*, that used to run through the nursery where the lake is today. He described how the Templais also caught a rich variety of fish in the Lot, a diversity long since lost.

Right: An early correspondent and customer of Latour-Marliac, Alphonse Karr wrote the introduction to *The Court of Flora* in which Nenuphar, or the white water lily, is portrayed in the guise of a nun.

Traces of blue can still be discerned on these ancient depictions of the Egyptian Blue Water Lily.

The Egyptian Blue Water Lily

The Sacred Blue Lotus or Egyptian Blue Water Lily, *N. caerulea*, can be seen in Ancient Egyptian paintings adorning the Nile and garden pools, being reverently inhaled or providing decorative motifs around and within many scenarios. It too rises from the muddy depths and was the symbol of the god Nefertem. In Egyptian mythology Nefertem was a lotus flower at the creation of the world, who rose from the primal depths accompanied by a sweet scent to represent the first sunlight. Depictions show him with a blue water lily headdress, a symbol of fragrance and beauty. His main cult centre was Memphis. Modern research has shown the blue water lily to have mild psycho-active properties which may account for its regular depictions at Ancient Egyptian parties or for sacramental use. In Channel 4's TV series, *Sacred Weeds*, an entire programme was dedicated to trialling its mind-altering effects on volunteers. Breeding hardiness into a blue water lily eluded Latour-Marliac but has now more or less been achieved. On the other hand, the Red Water Lily, *N. pubescens* and *N. rubra* proved to be easy to hybridise, the latter provided Latour-Marliac with one of the keys that unlocked his own psychedelic palette.

Left: The Sacred Blue Lotus or Egyptian Blue Water Lily, *Nymphaea caerulea*, in its blue and white forms was a major feature of Ancient Egyptian decoration.

Overleaf: *Nymphaea* caerulea.

CHAPTER 1
The Colours of the Orient brought to the Waters of the North

The Colours of the Orient brought to the Waters of the North

'...we owe a deep debt of gratitude to M. Latour-Marliac, who has given us an addition to our hardy garden flora which cannot be over estimated. He has added the large and noble forms and the soft and lovely colour of the Eastern water Lilies to the garden waters of northern countries. If this merely meant a gain of the beauty of the individual flower, our debt would be great and we would have good reason for gratitude but it is not only that. The splendid beauty of these plants will lead people to think of true and artistic ways of adorning garden waters... when people see that they may have in England the soft and beautiful yellow and the fine rose and red flowers of the tropical Water Lilies throughout summer and autumn, they will begin to take more interest in their water garden flowers'.

William Robinson, *The Garden*, 23rd December 1883

Botanical Identification

During the 19th century a global network of botanic gardens was established to identify the world's flora by name, and potential use. The dissemination of their findings was shared and discussed between professionals and educated amateurs.

One such professional was Joseph Decaisne (1807-1882), who started his botanical career in 1824 as gardener at the Muséum National d'Histoire Naturelle, Paris, rising to become head of the sowing section. He assisted Adrien-Henri de Jussieu who held the chair of rural botany, later to be President of the French Academy of Sciences, and key to much plant classification. Like Latour-Marliac, Decaisne's botanical studies were also practical, including agronomy and fruit growing, research on economic plants such as madder, yam and the ancient Chinese fibre plant, ramie. *

A legacy of 19th century empire building was the systematic recording of local flora. On 10th June 1863, the then Governor of Indochina, Admiral Pierre-Paul de La Grandière assigned L.A. Germain the task of directing work for

a zoo and botanical garden on twelve hectares of land sited near the Canal de l'Avanche, Scigon, now Thi Nghe canal, Ho Chi Min City. By the beginning of 1865 the site was planted up as a park and, in March La Grandière appointed the botanist Jean Baptiste Louis Pierre to be Director of The Saigon Botanic Garden, a post he held until 1877. In 1879 Charles Le Myre de Villers was appointed the *premier gouverneur civil de la Cochinchine* and *Ministre Plénipotentiaire* to the Court of Annam, before holding the post of *Député de la Cochinchine* from 1389-1902. It was with this corner of the French Empire that Latour-Marliac corresponded and where his son Édgard worked as Agent des Postes and plant hunted in the 1880s.

The trading of Europe's long established East India companies and the network of botanical gardens across the globe whetted appetites for exotic blooms and plant novelties. The proliferation of illustrated horticultural and gardening magazines allowed the rapid dissemination of news on the wonders of the plant world. A prolific writer and

---

*Ramie has been grown for its fibres for at least 7,000 years including for mummy cloths. The open weave fabric it produces inspired the French artist Raoul Dufy in the early 20th century and it is currently enjoying a revival as an 'ecological' fibre. In 1850, Decaisne was appointed Chair of Culture at the Muséum and in 1854 helped to found the Botanical Society of France. He described dozens of new plants, several in the Saururaceae family (*saura* – lizard, *oura* – tail) including *Gymnotheca chinensis* and *Saururus loureiri* both ordered by Monet from Latour-Marliac. His name appears in brackets sometimes as Decne.

founder of one of the foremost gardening magazines of the time, William Robinson was actively engaged, at times with some polemic and vitriol, but always with enthusiasm.

The grand gardens across Europe during the middle decades of the 19th century bedded out their generally

Italianate gardens with tender, colourful annual plants. The taste filtered down into public parks and small domestic gardens, where Robinson railed against the labour and the waste. He was in the vanguard of promoting and extending the Arts and Crafts philosophy into gardens that 'melted' into the countryside beyond. These gardens were planted with native trees and shrubs, complemented with hardy North American, Japanese and Chinese introductions, and delineated by borders of drifting perennial plants. In France, the drive to create natural beauty in and around cities using parks with lakes was promoted by Alexandre Godefroy-Lebeuf. This desire to make places green was matched by a strong criticism of the harshness of modern architecture, as exemplified by the Eiffel Tower.

During the 19th century, glass technology had advanced to such an extent that many European cities boasted fabulous winter gardens for which botanical collectors searched the globe in the quest to find exotic specimens to fill them. In 1845,

Previous spread: *Nymphaea* 'August Koch'. Apart from the rich violet-blue flowers, the long stems are the hallmark of tropical water lilies. In the 1890's Latour-Marliac supplied hardy water lilies for the parks of Chicago. This scented tropical, introduced in 1922, arose from a cross made at Garfield Park in Chicago by August Koch and George H Pring. Of all the tropical hues from which Latour-Marliac bred hardy equivalents, the blue proved to be elusive.

Above: Like many cities in temperate zones, the Palm House, here designed by Charles Lanyon in 1839 for Belfast's Botanic Garden, offered a propitious climate in which the local population could enjoy plants from around the world.

Right: A Japanese inspired rock pool with water lilies and marginal bamboos at Batsford Arboretum, Gloucestershire. A diplomatic career took Algernon Bertram Mitford, to Petersburg, China and then Japan as Second Secretary to the British Legation. In 1871 he wrote *Tales of Old Japan*. In 1886 he inherited Batsford House and estate (and added Freeman to his surname); he developed the landscape with Japanese and Chinese plants.

the gloriously illustrated journal *Flore des Serres et des Jardins de l'Europe* [*Flora of the Glasshouses and Gardens of Europe*] had been founded by the owner of the most successful nursery in Europe, Louis Van Houtte, based in Ghent. Like many nurserymen of the day, he sent out his own plant collectors to find orchids and other tropical and subtropical plants from South and Central America. Among those finds were tropical water lilies.

Van Houtte produced the first confirmed tropical water lily hybrid *Nymphaea* 'Ortgiesiano-rubra', which was named for its creator Eduard Ortgies. The seed had been obtained by Ortgies in Van Houtte's aquaria by removing stamens from the flower of *Nymphaea rubra* and dusting its stigma with the pollen of *Nymphaea ortgiesiana*. The result was a bright pink flower that opened wide, was more floriferous, but did not produce seeds. *N.* 'Ortgiesiano-rubra' was exhibited to the Horticultural Society (now Royal Horticultural Society) at Chiswick by Van Houtte in 1852. On his death in 1876 his son continued the nursery and Van Houtte went on to become one of Latour-Marliac's major customers.

Japonisme

In parallel with these trends in botany and landscaping was a growing taste for and fascination with the exoticism of the Orient. Magazines on the Arts and Crafts featured Japanese and Chinese fabrics, prints and silks. In this sense Monet's 1876 painting *La Japonaise*, or *Madame Monet in Japanese Costume* are emblematic of the period. Similar to Monet, Bory Latour-Marliac typified the educated, inquiring upper middle-class who both consumed and created the popular culture of the time. His family's wealth and agricultural businesses allowed him the funds and time to experiment scientifically, and the way in which he used that time captured the zeitgeist. For example, in the early years of his nursery, Latour-Marliac became a renowned expert on the importation of novel bamboo varieties from China and Japan.* What came next? Colourful water lilies floating on silky waters, often scented, hardy and available in sizes to suit all that had an even bigger public waiting in the wings to welcome them.

---

* In 1896 Sir A.B. Freeman-Mitford, Baron Redesdale), former British Ambassador to Japan, published *The Bamboo Garden*, and in its preface he acknowledges M Latour-Marliac, of Temple-sur-Lot, Lot-et-Garonne, France as 'the greatest European importer of these plants' who 'has always been most amiably ready to furnish me with the results of his observations'.

Joseph Bory Latour-Marliac and Le Temple-sur-Lot

'Such is the record of my labours amongst the Nymphaea. May my enthusiasm for the flora of the waters spread and induce many others to follow my example, in endeavouring to extend and enlarge the domain of horticulture.'

B. Latour-Marliac

To find the source of Joseph Bory Latour-Marliac's enthusiasm we must first look back at his forebears: Jean-Baptiste Geneviève Marcellin Bory de St Vincent, known as 'Bory,' had been born in the thriving town of Agen on 6th July 1778.* At the age of twenty he joined Captain Nicolas Baudin's expedition to Australia as a naturalist. In the event, he disembarked at Mauritius, he then spent a couple of years exploring islands in the Indian Ocean, developing his skills in botany and as a geographer. His good friend Léon Dufour paints a lively picture:

'I made my first acquaintance with Bory in 1802 on his return voyage from the islands of Bourbon and France, where he had left a scientific expedition led by Captain Baudin. We spent several months in arranging and classifying his new botanical conquests. During this work, he did not stop for a moment from singing and improvising couplets or making up rhymes on the scientific names of the plants that passed through our hands. He had a really comic talent for this.'

Following these botanical excursions, Bory de St Vincent returned to mainland France to join the army, seeing action at the Battle of Ulm and at Austerlitz as Captain of the Dragoons. He went subsequently to Spain in 1808 with Marshal Soult, eventually becoming *Attaché d'Etat Major* to Napoleon's 6th Army. His unswerving loyalty to Napoleon against the Bourbons in 1815 led to his exile until 1820. In 1829 he headed a scientific expedition to the Peloponnese and ten years later an exploration of Algeria.

By the time he had returned from Algeria he had become Deputy Colonel of the Lot-et-Garonne and a *Membre correspondant* of the Académie des Sciences, Paris. His wife was from Rennes, and together they had two daughters, but no son on whom to pass his name.**

On 6th March 1830, Bory de St Vincent's cousin, Joseph Bory Latour-Marliac, was born to the mayor of the Commune of Granges-sur-Lot, Guillaume Latour-Marliac and his wife Victorine (*née* de St Vincent). Granges-sur-Lot is a town some 20 miles north of Agen, where the Latour-Marliac family had a house they referred to as Château le Rouge.†

---

*The town of Agen had enjoyed a building boom during the mid 18th century, which was followed by an intellectual renaissance after the 1789 Revolution. The northerly tides of France's Atlantic coast and the southerly seas of its Mediterranean coast were ambitiously joined by the Canal des Deux Mers. The project was conceived and started by Louis Vauban in the 1680s, but was not completed until 1856 – just as the railways arrived. During 1839 the canal was carried over the River Garonne in Agen, midway between Bordeaux and Toulouse.

**Dufour records that Bory rarely mentioned his wife but was a popular society figure surrounded by fun and laughter. The Byronic, or should I say, Napoleonic portrait of him overleaf is attractively romantic and dashing. Between 1802 and 1838 he published five works that described the Canary Islands, Islands of Africa, Caves of Maastricht and a geography of the Iberian peninsula as well as *Man: a Zoological Essay on the Human Species*. One can imagine that such a talented traveller returning to Agen for his final years would have enlivened many a social and family gathering with his charm, intellectual rigour, literary skills and ability to sing.

† Victorine's father and grandfather were important legal figures in Agen, with Bory de St Vincent her father's first cousin. An ornamental metal cross stands on a stone plinth in the churchyard of the small town of Granges-sur-Lot. A plaque is dedicated to its curé Jacques-Daniel Latour-Marliac (1733-1805). It records that he was born on the Ile de Saint-Domingue, present day Haiti. The family fled the island in 1803, which at the time was convulsed with an ever more violent succession of slave rebellions, to return to the safety of their roots. Little could they imagine that his priestly tenure between 1771 and 1805 would witness the French Revolution, the Terror, and conversion of churches into Temples of Reason. His brother, Jean, married Jeanne Rigaud de Jenouilhac, their son Pierre was born on the Ile de Saint-Domingue. Pierre married Marie-Thèrese de Bonseigneur, and it was their son Guillaume and his wife Victorine who built up an extensive estate of plum orchards, vineyards and property in the vicinity. As they prospered, winters were passed in civilised fashion amongst the cosmopolitan society of Bordeaux with the magnificent Grand Theatre de Bordeaux at its cultural heart.

Facing page: The waters from the Latour-Marliac nursery flow into this canal. Le Temple-sur-Lot suffered regular flooding until the 1950s when diversionary schemes were undertaken. Writing to Charles Ellis in March 1897, Latour-Marliac recorded that they had suffered the wettest winter for a century. The River Lot had risen some 45 feet and flooded all his *bassins*.

Bory de St. Vincent 1778-1846

Once he was old enough, the young Joseph Bory Latour-Marliac stayed with his grandparents so that he could attend school in Agen. Perhaps his adventuring cousin's books were on their shelves; the young namesake would have surely relished the tales of botanical derring-do. Indeed, Bory de St Vincent loomed large in Bory Latour-Marliac's life, as some of his correspondence decades later reveals. Writing to the Comte de Castillon in 1888, he explained the origin of his name:

'Here is the explanation: Bory de St. Vincent, first cousin of Bory my maternal grandfather, had only daughters – his name would be lost to posterity; so it was that from birth all the family convened to award me with the name of Bory to stop it dying out; and since then it has been my usual name within the family. When I entered in horticultural operations I did not wish to use this name associated with academic botanical papers on a banal catalogue, and so it was only after having obtained some plants of distinction that I made up my mind to use it in my horticultural transactions.'

It was, in other words, a name to live up to, at least in horticultural terms.*

Upon earning his *baccalauréat* a Agen, the young Latour-Marliac was sent to study law in Paris around 1847. His namesake cousin had died in December 1846. One may speculate that Bory de St Vincent's reputation would have opened doors into the capital's scientific and botanical societies for Latour-Marliac. According to Latour-Marliac's great-great grandson Guillaume Laydeker, Bory de St Vincent had been a Director of the Natural History Museum in Paris. However, official records show otherwise. Amongst many works he was a founder member of France's *Société entomologique* and principal editor of the *Dictionnaire classique d'histoire naturelle*. Both sides of the family shared

---

* When Latour-Marliac was a schoolboy in Agen, the Comtes de Castillon were the social pinnacle of the large south-westerly region of Aquitaine, their name celebrated in Castillon-La-Bataille, the site of the last battle of the Hundred Years War with the English, and the wines of the Cote de Castillon. Bory's 'entry into horticultural operations' as an adult eventually led to years of regular correspondence with and orders for bamboo from the then Comte de Castillon. The correspondence began in the 1870s, and in 1881 they discussed the Bordeaux region's problems with *phylloxera*, speculating about available grape varieties and research in the United States. They also discussed the introduction of American rootstock, which would ultimately be used to resurrect the region's decimated vineyards.

An aerial view of the River Lot, village of Le Temple-sur-Lot and Latour-Marliac Nursery. The nursery is outlined in white and surrounded by orchards.

an interest in botany and horticulture, with Latour-Marliac's father Guillaume publishing pamphlets on local and Mediterranean flora between 1830 and 1850, and it was around this family legacy rather than the law, that his life's work would soon start to burgeon.

In February 1848 the next revolutionary wave that was to engulf Europe and parts of South America rose in the French capital with the bloody suppression of the June Days Uprising. Latour-Marliac was forced to return home, where he worked on the family estate, engaged in botanical pursuits, and married Alida Gonnère in 1852. They had two children, Angéle and Édgard, and set up home in Le Temple-sur-Lot. Only Angéle would marry to a Monsieur Maurice Laydeker. Water lily *connoisseurs* will know these names because they are memorialised in the horticultural nomenclature associated with water lilies as 'Marliacea' and 'Laydekeri'.

The collecting and hybridising of tropical water lilies undertaken by Van Houtte and others was inspirational for Latour-Marliac. He stated as much in his 1887 article, *Des Nymphaea et Nelumbium Rustiques*, in which he quotes at length words written by Charles Lemaire, the eminent French botanist and first editor of Van Houtte's journal.

'Obtaining hardy *Nymphaea* from hybridisation with tropical species has long been the objective of numerous experiments. In this regard we read in an 1854 edition of the 'Jardin Botaniste', published in Belgium, the following article on the *Nymphaea Devoniensis* [by Charles Lemaire]: "Would it not be a wonderful thing that a new race could be obtained for example by crossing our *N. alba* with blue or red flowered *Nymphaea*?"'

Above: Victoria sp. Eduard Ortgies worked at Chatsworth from 1849 to 1850. That year could not have been more timely as he gained first hand experience of working in Joseph Paxton's innovative Stove House and helped Paxton raise the first *Victoria regia*. Paxton had collected the four leaved seedling from Kew on his 46th birthday, 3rd August 1849, and returned with it by express train. To date no-one had succeeded in growing a *Victoria* so the race was on and Paxton's team was soon leading the field. On the evening of 8th November the purest white flower elegantly and sweetly rose out of the water, she gave a repeat performance for the next three nights. Paxton personally took a blossom to Queen Victoria and the great botanists William Hooker, John Lindley and George Bentham beat a hasty track to Chatsworth. Ortgies had proved to be a talented gardener and with glowing references he moved to the Van Houtte nurseries in 1850. Here he crossed *Nymphaea dentata* with *N. rubra*, and the resultant cross was named for him *Nymphaea* 'Ortgiesiano-rubra'.

And later this eloquent exclamation:

"What a splendid spectacle, a vast aquarium where *N. caerulea, scutifolia, dentata, lotus, gigantea, gracilis, odorata, pygmaea, ampla*, etc. were scattered across its surface and all flowering; along with *Victoria regia* or *cruziana; Euryale ferox, Nelumbium capsicum, speciosum, luteum*, etc.: all with full floating or emergent leaves, with superb, large flowers of white, blue, red, pink yellow, etc. Amongst these plants would be *Lymnocharis, Pontederia, Aponogeton, Caladium, Colocasia*, etc., etc., and exclaim: is it not the most grandiose, most admirable, most attractive spectacle in the world." Today the knowledgeable author of these lines, M. Ch. Lemaire would be overjoyed to see such a ravishing perspective outside a heated greenhouse.'

When Lemaire's article was published in 1854, Latour-Marliac had read it and been captivated by the sensuous and colourful dream of aquatic flora that it described. He would later say that it marked the initiation of his hybridising ambition. Apart from improving his orchard trees, he started importing and collecting bamboo. Work on water lilies soon followed. In 1875 he founded a specialist nursery surrounded by plum and almond orchards or four hectares in Le Temple-sur-Lot, site of the ancient *Commanderie de l'Ordre du Temple*, known in English as the Knights Templar. A propitious location for both bamboo and aquatic plants the parcel of land was running with water, crossed as it was by a stream, dotted by fourteen quasi-thermal springs, and anchored by two productive wells that tapped into the region's shallow and abundant sandstone aquifers. It was here where Latour-Marliac would build the company and create the plants that would carry his name into the next two centuries.

The Hybridiser's Palette emerges, and with it a New Enterprise

'I applied myself to the object of effecting a cross which should produce plants with bright-red flowers much finer in colour, to N. sphaerocarpa. … I have obtained some remarkably hardy novelties which for six months of the year embellish the waters of pleasure grounds with their splendid flowers. Most of them are catalogued as N. Robinsonii, Seignoureti, Laydekeri, rosea, liliacea, fulgens, Marliacea, ignea, N.M. rubra punctata and N.M. flammea. Others no less brilliant will soon be added to the list.'

B. Latour-Marliac, *The Garden*, 1893

The records of everything Latour-Marliac wrote; letters both professional and personal, orders and articles, have survived on thin, translucent 'onion-skin' paper in bound volumes of 500 pages. There are 34 surviving volumes dating from 1881 to 1924. The first is dated 19th February 1881. In it he thanks Monsieur Langlois of Neufchateau for his order of aquatic plants, including Nelumbium and Nuphar, which were to be despatched from the end of March. He noted the customer's interest in Nuphar avena with an orange heart. The last volume is incomplete, without index, and its correspondence is all signed 'Laydeker'. The last entry is dated the 21st December 1924 and addressed to Perry's Hardy Plant Farm.

Many early letters, between Latour-Marliac and other horticultural specialists, give an insight of how he undertook the creation of his new water lily varieties. It is important to note that the precise method he used to make his crosses remains unknown, but my archival work has unearthed new information that gives a more accurate picture. What we

Below: *Nymphaea* 'Laydekeri Lilacea' was introduced in 1893 and remains a beautiful small water lily. The flowers open as a rose-pink, gently darkening to carmine as they mature with a mass of sparkling stamens.

know now is that Latour-Marliac's palette, which is to say the pollen and seed parent* plants he used to make his crosses, consisted of many different water lilies from around the world.

When Latour-Marliac began his hybridising work, the hardy water lily in Europe consisted of the white species *Nymphaea alba*, which grows naturally in lakes, ponds and slow-moving rivers. The different shapes and colours that Latour-Marliac ultimately created came from a variety of hardy, tropical and subtropical water lily species. Latour-Marliac's pinks and reds, for example, appear to have come from a tropical species and two naturally occurring hardy mutations. *Nymphaea rubra*, referred to by Latour-Marliac as

'*rubra* des Indes' or rubra from the Indies, is a red tropical species found throughout the warmest regions of Asia. *Nymphaea alba rubra* (also known as *Nymphaea* 'Caspary' in honour of the German botanist Dr Robert Caspary, who noted nine variations of *N. alba*) is a red genetic mutation of the otherwise white *N. alba*. In Latour-Marliac's day, these plants had only recently been discovered growing in a remote lake in Sweden.** There are numerous mentions of *N. caspary* or *alba rubra* scattered throughout the archives, many of which show admiration toward the 'Swedish mutation' but a denial that it was a source of the red in his varieties.

A genetic mutation had also occurred in the white water lily native to North America, *Nymphaea odorata*. That

---

*In hybridising terms, the pollen parent is the plant that furnishes the male reproductive material, while the seed or pistillate parent is the one that furnishes the female material i.e. the fertile womb. When making a cross, the hybridiser takes the pollen from a plant with desirable characteristics and applies it to the pistil, or female reproductive part, of another plant. Each seedling produced from the match will be a unique combination of traits

from the parent plants. The diligent hybridiser is a patient one, germinating the seedlings and bringing them to flower in order to decide which plants are worth keeping and potentially naming.

**Today, the native red water lilies of Lake Fagertärn, in the Tiveden National Park, are protected.

Facing page: *Nymphaea gigantea.* 1900 was a busy year for James Hudson, gardener to Leopold de Rothschild, who had built up an outstanding reputation not least for raising tropical water lilies. Unfortunately Latour-Marliac was unable to fulfill his requests owing to the *Exposition Universelle* in Paris. On 28th July 1900 the *Gardeners' Chronicle* featured a *Nymphaea gigantea*: 'Our illustration was taken from a flower exhibited by Mr Hudson at the Drill Hall ... a native of Queensland'. It was the winner of the RHS First Class Certificate. Later that year Hudson wrote a report on another blue water lily, *N. stellata* var *pulcherrima,* which appeared on 13th October.

Below: Europe's native hardy white water lily, *Nymphaea alba,* poetic but not colourful.

variation, known as *N. odorata rubra* was found growing in a kettle pond on Cape Cod in Massachusetts. The hardy Rubras were exceedingly rare and took Latour-Marliac years and much negotiation to procure. Having obtained them he claims not to have used them to any great extent for a variety of reasons, preferring instead the outcomes of more elaborate 'intersubgeneric' hybridisation i.e. crosses with a subgenus [or subdivision] of the genus *Nymphaea.* A time-consuming process of artificially crossing the tropical *N. rubra* with the hardy *N.odorata rubra* and then crossing those first generation plants with others. *N. flava* and *N. mexicana* are two strains of the subtropical yellow water lily that grows in Florida's Lake Okeechobee. Latour-Marliac learned of these plants, and was able to obtain them, largely as the result of his horticultural network that spanned the globe. He used *N. mexicana* for yellow and copper tints.

A first generation hybrid, *N.* 'Laydekeri Grandiflora' was used to yield a number of sterile second generation plants. That such a process was used is borne out by the fact that many of Latour-Marliac's hybrids are known to be sterile i.e. they do not produce seed a trait that is commonly associated with second-generation plant hybrids. This was a desirable characteristic fo Latour-Marliac in both commercial and horticultural terms. In the first case, sterile plants that could only be reproduced via division of the rhizome ensured that his clients and competitors would not be able to create new colourful varieties from crosses made with his plants. It also gave him a virtual monopoly on the creation of colourful hardy water lilies, if not on their cultivation, and one that would last for nearly 100 years. In the second case, it also guaranteed that his plants would remain pure in perpetuity.*

Spontaneous new plants are as a result of natural rather than artificial pollination or mutation, a naturally occurring morphological or chemical change in a plant. What is imperative in any of these operations or their outcomes is skilled botanical observation and interpretation.

The written evidence

Latour-Marliac's work on hybridising water lilies enters the archives on 29th May 1882, when he sent a little box of the tender *Nymphaea scutifolia* with blue flowers to a Madame Laflon in Machetaux. He noted with disappointment that the *Nymphaea* with red flowers had not *rejetonné* (sprouted new crowns), however, if and when it did, he would send one. Latour-Marliac's deft networking skills cannot be over-estimated for the role that they played in his ability to procure the plants he needed to complete his palette, and eventually to commercialise the results of his crosses. This is illustrated in his next letter to a Madame Laflon in July, in which he discusses his efforts at creating a yellow hardy water lily:

'For a long time the colours blue, pink and red were known already in the genus *Nymphaea*, but the colour of pure yellow was only found in the Lotus genus whose simple flowers only have five petals.

Today the quest is on for a true *Nymphaea* with double yellow flowers; a novelty and precious conquest from which in the future without doubt will result hybrids with flowers washed with yellow, red and blue.

I have pleasure in sending you the first flowers of a young root from this magnificent Nymphaea of which M Philippe has spoken to me and which you have received from New York.

Would you be so kind as to drop me a quick line to let me know if I should save you a cutting. I beg you also to give me (not unless you have some interest in keeping it or not telling it) the address of that New York horticulturist who seemed to me to be well acquainted and to whom I could make an order from which you would also benefit. Finally could you save me some seeds of yellow *Nelumbium* for me to send to one of my friends, if you have some to spare.

I express to you, Madame, all the pain that I share with you following the hail which destroyed your crops and send you my respects and warm salutations.'

(22nd July, 1882)

Over the years Latour-Marliac frequently put a postscript down the side of the paper and this letter was no exception: 'The yellow *Nymphaea* is growing outdoors'. It is in fact a common misconception that the yellow hardy water lily has always existed in nature, like the white water lily. This is probably due to the genus Nuphar, commonly known as pond lily, which grows throughout Europe and North America, and which has large floating leaves and tiny, bud-like yellow flowers. A few years after his letter to Madame Laflon, Latour-Marliac would succeed in creating the first true yellow water lily, known as *Nymphaea* 'Marliacea Chromatella'.

N. odorata rubra, or the pink mutation of *Nymphaea odorata* found in Cape Cod, is also mentioned in a number of letters in the archives. One of the first can be found in a letter to a Monsieur Gétrand of Barbezieux in the Poitou-Charente region. After opening paragraphs on bamboo and the difficulties of growing *Nelumbium*, Latour-Marliac informed Gétrand that he now had 15 varieties of hardy water lilies, details of which he would send in the spring. He goes on:

'Finally, you will be interested by the most beautiful of all, a novelty also from a hardy source, the water lily or *Nymphaea odorata rubra*! With a red, scented flower which I have not yet put on sale and which I reckon will be 30F each ... It is certain that nothing surpasses the beauty of a stretch of water or aquarium decorated with *Nymphaeas* and *Nelumbiums* [Lotus]. In closing, Monsieur, I respond to your astonishment that I had knowledge of your standing as a horticultural amateur, with the fact that my numerous contacts allow me to find the addresses of the principal serious and distinguished professionals and amateurs in agriculture and horticulture in every department ...' (4th September, 1882)

Latour-Marliac's acquisition of *odorata rubra* was again the result of consistent and constructive networking. Writing to Godefroy-Lebeuf who had sent him a copy of *The American Garden*, Latour-Marliac tells the story of how he was able to procure them:

'The *Nymphaea odorata rubra* is a plant that I received from America through the intermediary of the doyen of American horticulturists, Mr Hovey. He was here in 1878 and saw a flowering *Nymphaea* 'Caspary' at my place. He told me that near Boston there was a variety with flowers of such a brilliant pink, that those flowers were sold at a dollar apiece and that the monopoly was in the hands of one of his neighbours, who had never been willing to sell the plant. Mr Hovey asserted that on no account would this neighbour part with his goose that lays the golden eggs. I urged him to try the deal and put a thousand francs at his disposal. After a few months I received five or six plants as my share and Mr Hovey kept the rest.' (19th August, 1888)

Three key events in his achievement as a hybridiser are revealed in 1887 – a paper, introductions to Kew and William Robinson. *Notice sur les Nymphaea & Nelumbium Rustiques – Leur culture et celle d'autres plantes aquatiques* [Paper on Hardy Nymphaea & Nelumbium – Their culture and that of other aquatic plants], described his work and the ease with which hardy water lilies could be grown. In a way

Facing page: In 1892 Latour-Marliac entered into lengthy correspondence with Mr R. H. Faunce of Sandwich, which lies at the westerly side of Cape Cod. Cape Cod's Kettle Ponds were formed some 13,000 to 15,000 years ago as the great glaciers were retreating. Huge blocks of ice were left behind that formed holes, as the temperatures continued to rise they filled with water. A hardy red mutation *N. odorata rubra* was discovered here. Today there are twenty permanently flooded freshwater ponds within the Cape Cod National Seashore ranging from one to 44 hectares.

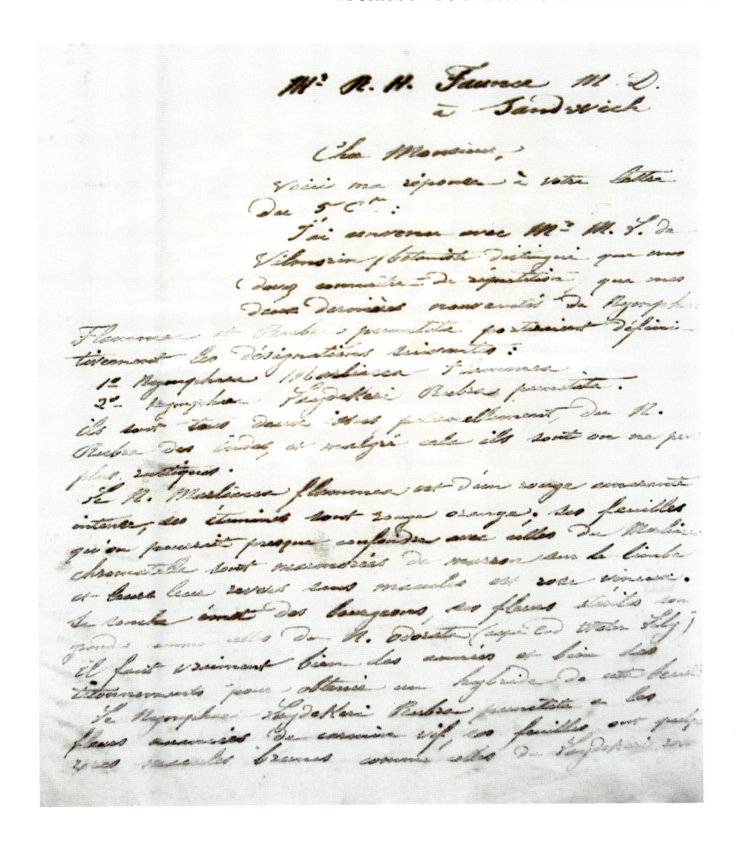

that surely ascertains his annual winter season at Bordeaux's Grand Theatre, he describes N. 'Caspary' from Sweden and compares it to its tropical cousin, N. rubra:

'Like its compatriot, Offenbach's hero in La Vie Parisienne, it has made its entry into the horticultural world accompanied by a grand orchestra and a lot of fuss. It is cloaked in carmine to look like N. rubra, but this has not been a complete success so it has adopted a misleading red. The leaves are large, entire, veined at the base and sometimes wavy around the edges. The average sized floating flowers are white on the outside and inside a carmine pink. They flower from June to September'.

The Royal Botanic Garden at Kew was amongst the most prestigious in the world, and it was to that august place that Latour-Marliac sent one of his first cuttings of 'Chromatella'. On 6th June 1887 he addressed himself to George Nicholson at Kew, enclosing an example of a leaf and flower from the yellow *Nymphaea* 'Marliacea Chromatella' and a flower of the *Nymphaea odorata rubra*. Latour-Marliac asked whether Nicholson might like to send a plant of *Nymphaea scutifolia* with blue flowers in exchange for his *Nymphaea odorata rubra*. Latour-Marliac suggested protecting the plants in the post by wrapping them in moist moss. On 6th July Latour-Marliac also sent one each of *Nymphaea* 'Marliacea Chromatella', *Nymphaea* 'Marliacea Chromatella Foliis Hepatiis Marmoratis', *Nymphaea odorata rubra* (bright pink), and *Nymphaea* 'Odorata Rosacea' (baby pink). He assured Nicholson that they were all hardy and very remarkable. On 28th April 1888 Latour-Marliac promised to send *Nymphaea* 'Voalefoka de Madagascar' and an *N.* 'odorata sulphurea rosacea' (of his own breeding) and flava. They were also in touch regarding bamboos. In 1889 Nicholson provided the addresses of horticulturists in New Zealand and was asked to save some seeds of *N. zanzibariensis*, followed a week later by a further request for the seeds of a small cucumber. In

September 1892 Latour-Marliac sent a large bamboo selection (bamboo remained the primary interest into 1894 and 1895) and a small package of *Nymphaea*. The interest in *Nymphaea* was revived in April 1897 with five each of 'Marliacea Carnea', 'Caroliniana' followed in August by *N. zanzibariensis*.

On 13th July 1887 he started his correspondence with William Robinson in England. In his second letter, dated 21st July, Latour-Marliac explained the haphazard way in which he undertook some of his first crosses, making it difficult to determine the exact parentage. Essentially, he took whatever white hardy species he cultivated 'the alba – the Candida (from Bohemia) – the tuberosa – the odorata – the odorata minor (these last three from Northern America) and a great number of other species mixed with red, blue, etc. Nymphaeas from the Tropics'. Although he was unable to assign exact botanical parentage, he classed all outcomes as 'Castalia'. In an article he submitted to Robinson, for publication in an 1893 issue of *The Garden*, Latour-Marliac explained that the resulting crosses were not stable, but yielded pollen for further hybridisation. He wrote that these '… varieties, which it is impossible to render permanent, owing to the failure of their rhizomes to yield offsets, have proved very useful for hybridising choice varieties of the stoloniferous and proliferous kinds; and from these I have obtained some remarkably hardy novelties …' That year he corrected Robinson regarding his crosses:

'I have never wished to use the *N.* Sphaerocarpa (N. Caspary or alba rubra) for my artificial raisings, noting that they were neither sufficiently floriferous nor red in colour. I used to prefer *N.* rubra des indes …'

This statement again undermines the erroneous belief that the red found in Latour-Marliac's hybrids came from *N. alba rubra*, but as outlined above from hardy yet transient intersubgeneric hybrids that were created by crossing the tropical *N. rubra* with hardy species. These first generation crosses did not survive, but they did last long enough to produce pollen. These initial crosses were then used as vehicles by Latour-Marliac to create the varieties we know today.

Fifteen years later, in response to a letter dated 14th July 1902 from Julien Chifflot of Lyon, Latour-Marliac wrote: '… I inform you that in my hybridisation I have never used *N. alba-rosea* (Caspary) because of its parsimonious flowering and the overwhelming inferiority of the magnificent seed pods that I have obtained and which I have never given over to commerce.' In a later letter that was part of the same exchange, Latour-Marliac reiterated his stance on

B. LATOUR-MARLIAC.

Facing page: Cover of the earliest surviving catalogue of 1882. Latour-Marliac styles himself as horticulturist and a member of the Royal Linnean Society of Brussels. Inside 14 different species of *Nymphaea* are offered – *alba plena*, 'Carnea', 'Caspary', *flava*, *lotus*, *minor odorata*, *odorata*, *ortegesiana rubra*, *poecile*, *pygmaea*, *rubra*, *thermalis*, *tuberosa* and *scutifolia*.

On page seven, he lists two *Nuphar* – *advena* at 5 francs each and *lutea* 1 franc 50. Under *Nymphaea* he mixes the subtropical *Nelumbium* and hardy water lilies, listing them in alphabetical order with a small 'c' to indicate 'chaud' (warmth) is required. All were readily available.

Above: Summer in Le Temple-sur-Lot comes to an abrupt end with a heavy frost, usually in October. Latour-Marliac was able to overwinter the more tender Lotus, *Nelumbium,* in their *bassin* although an especially harsh winter would kill them. He created more sheltered environments using the thermal springs near the *Ruisseau de la Grésille* and glass covers for his tender plants.

Right: Bory Latour-Marliac was delighted by this engraving used by William Robinson in the 1893 volume of *The Garden*.

Above: An original illustration of the *Nymphaea* 'Carnea', 'Ignea' and 'Chromatella' dating from the late 1880s.

Left above: *Nymphaea* 'Marliacea Chromatella',** note the attractively distinctive mottling on the leaves. It was one of Latour-Marliac's enduring favourite water lilies. Examples were also sent to George Nicholson at Kew along with the fleshy pink coloured *N.* 'Marliacea Carnea'.

Left centre: *Nymphaea* 'Marliacea Carnea'. New to the 1882 catalogue, Latour-Marliac charged 12 francs for these plants.

Left bottom: *Nymphaea* 'Marliacea Ignea' was introduced in 1893. *Ignea* is derived from the Latin for fiery red. It is one of what Latour-Marliac described perfectly as 'remarkably hardy novelties which for six months of the year embellish the waters of pleasure grounds with their splendid flowers'.

N. 'Caspary': 'As I told you, I have never been able to use Caspary's N. 'Sphaerocarpa' (*alba rubra*) for my breeding and it is easy to be convinced by an examination of the more or less red colour of my hybrid's stamens which fall into carmines, amaranths, etc. On the other hand, it is worth noticing that during the flowers' fading phases they need the Rubra des Indes to augment the colour intensity and this can be provided by crossing with the odorata rosea, or rubra of the type'. He said he doubted that this would take place spontaneously, and that he had also used odorata rubra to create varieties such as N. Caroliniana – N. Caroliniana perfecta – Marliacea carnea – N. Rosea, etc.' In the catalogue he had marked the *Nymphaea* that were seed bearing with an X.

In the same correspondence he explains the process more precisely with regard to his creation of *Nymphaea* 'Fulva,' a coppery variety with red-mottled pads. 'The N. 'Fulva' is the product of a 'Laydekeri' with very large flowers and that of Florida Flava which can only be distinguished from *mexicana* by its more tapering petals. I will send you a flower in the first fortnight of September as a specimen of this 'Laydekeri grandiflora', issue of a cross between the exotic N. extra-tropical and the Rubra des Indes' [presumably a triple cross using a 'Laydekeri']. He closed with the promise of sending some flowers of equally remarkable new hybrids as well. By 23rd September he wrote to say a parcel had been despatched two days earlier including: '... the seed head of N. Laydekeri grandiflora, which I would like you to know,

and one of its varieties, with a clearer tone, equally with a seedhead. Finally, three superb hybrids, sterile, issues from Laydekeri grandiflora.' 'Laydekeri Grandiflora', being a fragile first generation cross, no longer exists, but a number of its progeny do. In addition to *N*. 'Fulva', the three 'superb' but as yet unnamed other hybrids alluded to are likely to be among *N*. 'Indiana', *N*. 'Seignoureti', *N*. 'Aurora' and *N*. 'Robinsonii'. While rare, these varieties still exist and remain in cultivation.

Commercial and scientific publication

The earliest commercial catalogue in the archives is dated 1882 and adopts the rather oriental presentation of the unhyphenated name Latour Marliac and no mention of Bory. This is presumably what he meant by a 'banal' catalogue

when writing to Castillon. It recods that he is a member of the Royal Linnean Society of Brussel and a Horticulturist who specialises in aquatic and bog plars. Curiously, of all the plants stocked he and/or his printer chose roses to illustrate the title page. Although the 188 -1383 archives are dominated by bamboo sales and a growing interest in aquatics, it does also record severa purchases and sales of roses. There are nonetheless 14 varieties of *Nymphaea* listed in the 1882 catalogue. The pastel hues of pale pink and yellow are offered at prices betwee 3 and 5 francs, the common white at 1 franc 50, bu the new hardy hybrid *N*. Carnea and the newly discovered species *N*. Caspary (alba rubra) are both 12 francs each.

Five years later, on 24th March 887, Latour-Marliac had written to thank Godefroy-Lebeu for the copy of his new

*The bi-monthly magazine *Le Jardin* was launched in 1887 with the opening words:

'Never before has the taste for flowers, for plants been so general: they preside over every ceremony, they are at all our festivals, their consummation has increased one hundred fold over the last twenty years and their industrial culture has become a profitable source for many formerly disinherited regions'.

It was founded by the aforementioned Alexandre Godefroy-Lebeuf in Argenteuil, who came from a long line of horticulturists and botanists. As dealers in exotic plants, one of the family's 18th century creations had been an exotic colonial garden at the site of the chateau des Brouillards, on the

impasse des Brouillards in Montmartre. A hunced years later Renoir described the neglected gardens as:

'A mysterious, stately garden, like Zola's paradou – what was once part of a fine residence'.

One painting captures the voluptuous uncontrolled garden with reputedly Monet and Alfred Sisley in the background. An Impressionist link with Godefroy-Lebeuf was established when Gustave Caillebotte introduced him to Monet when they all lived in Argenteuil for several years, and also with the author Octave Mirbeau. These were all regular subscribers to *Le Jardin* and Mirbeau even contributed to one of God -froy-Lebeuf's other specialist magazines *L'Orchidophile* [The Orchid Lover]

Facing page: *N. mexicana*. As its name suggests it originates in Mexico, as well as Florida's Lake Okeechobee.

Below: *Nymphaea odorata rubra*. In 1882 Latour-Marliac described this as the most beautiful water lily of all.

journal, *Le Jardin*, but was disappointed that there were no colour plates.* He confirmed that he would be happy to write a fairly lengthy treatise on aquatic plants for a volume that would give their name, family, culture, botanical description, temperament, etc. preferably in alphabetic order. He suggested that in order to keep the contents up to date and with added interest he would regularly contribute additional articles that specialised in new plants of merit, particularly *Nymphaea* and *Nelumbium*. He had obtained hybrid *Nymphaea* of the greatest beauty, he said, the flowers and leaves of which he would send as soon as they started flowering. He had enclosed his latest catalogue and a payment of 12 francs for the new journal. He signed off with

a PS asking Godefroy-Lebeuf to send him 100 seeds of Pansies *à grandes maules* which sound very blousy!

Latour-Marliac's disappointment that *Le Jardin* was not illustrated was short lived as, by April 1888, he had made arrangements for Mlle Jeanne Koch to paint water lily novelties for the magazine. By the end of May, flowers and pads of *N.* 'Marliacea' had been sent to the 'accomplished' Mlle Koch, and this continued through June. The correspondence between Latour-Marliac and Godefroy-Lebeuf continued in the build up to and during the 1889 Paris *Exposition Universelle*, in which both men were actively involved.

Godefroy-Lebeuf had commissioned an article on the *Nymphaea* 'Marliacea chromatella foliis marmoratis', which had been sent to George Nicholson at the Royal Botanic Gardens at Kew. On 28th January 1889 he requested a chromo lithograph of the Latour-Marliac family and on 17th February engravings were sent. By the end of 1889 Latour-Marliac could look back on an international triumph, which his future order books and global contacts would reflect.

Country Life in 19th and Early 20th Century Lot-et-Garonne

The family and its welfare had always been of paramount importance to Joseph Bory and Alida Latour-Marliac. Their children and grandchildren were kept abreast of all developments and their financial interests were just as carefully nurtured. Henri Laydeker, in an undated fax from the 1990s, wrote that the Latour-Marliacs owned seventeen familial properties in Le Temple, Granges-sur-Lot, Saint Sardos and other villages. Following in his father's footsteps, Latour-Marliac was involved in local affairs and stood as Mayor of Le Temple in 1895. Their life was by all accounts comfortable and idyllic. They spent winters in Bordeaux and during the summer they lived in many ways as squires of their country manor, one surrounded by water lilies. Latour-Marliac seemed to relish country living, taking great satisfaction in the fruits, vegetables and cuisine that the Lot-et-Garonne provided in abundance.

There are really only three seasons at Le Temple-sur-Lot – spring, summer and winter, essentially the summer continues through September until it is brought to an abrupt halt with a hard frost in October. After one or two frosts the leaves fall leaving the countryside with a bare, bleak look traversed by slow bodies of water. Climatic patterns seasoned Latour-Marliac's order acknowledgements, letters and articles. These records provide a valuable historic insight into local weather conditions. For example, the late May frost of 1881 killed his *nelumbium*, leaving them in a pitiable state and delaying the production of his other plants. In September that year, he wrote to M Le Comte [de Castillon] that it had been raining in torrents since yesterday. The winter of 1887/1888 was one of extreme frosts but undaunted, Latour-Marliac wrote cheerfully that it was always interesting to see what would be the outcome.

Facing page: Although the family home with its gardens and lily pond is still owned by his descendents, the house is mostly boarded up, but still furnished.

Right: The village of Le Temple-sur-Lot is still surrounded by fruit orchards, seen here at dawn in the spring. The plum trees provide fruit that is suitable for drying as prunes, a local speciality much prized.

Below: An undated late 19th or early 20th century black and white photograph entitled 'Cote Midi' [South Side]. Is it Latour-Marliac sitting under the shade of the tree on the left hand side? The *bassins* are full of water lilies and the site well-maintained.

Above: A view across the original *bassins* built by Latour-Marliac in the 1870s that now hold the French National Water Lily Collection.

Facing page: The Strawn collection in the Latour-Marliac exhibit on pools. In the background, *Iris ensata* in full bloom. A dazzling effect on a sunny summer's day – flowers reaching up to the sun and leaves burnished by it. Monet was captivated by the sensations of light on water lilies and irises.

The traces of their lifestyle have been preserved in the archive, but also in the places they once inhabited.

Oral history places the Latour-Marliac family living in Granges-sur-Lot during the 19th century, presumably after their flight from Ile de Domingue in 1803. After 1875 it appears that Bory and Alida Latour-Marliac lived in their spacious townhouse in Le Temple-sur-Lot, which is a five-minute walk from the nursery. According to his great-great-grandson Bory Laydeker, that house was built in the early 1800s with money granted by Napoleon to aristocratic families who had been displaced, disowned, or otherwise affected by the revolution of 1789. The house is still the most prominent in the village and would have been magnificent in its day, consisting of four storeys plus servants' quarters and a spacious attic in the fifth storey. Still owned by the Laydeker family, but rarely visited by them, the Latour-Marliac house in Le Temple-sur-Lot is traditional and grand with its most attractive façade overlooking the plane tree-lined street leading to the village centre. Today the interior of the house and its gardens leave an eerie impression as

though Bory and Alida Latour-Marliac simply packed up and left one day 100 years ago. The wall treatments, fixtures and furniture seem unchanged from their era, except everything is now faded, cracking and peeling with age The dusty attic is filled with wooden crates and the bric-a-brac of another epoque, with the silken webs of its current inhabitants industrially decorating every perceivable nook and cranny. In an old reading room, yellowed, leather-bound tomes lie here and there on surfaces and shelves, and a rocking chair sits poised in the corner; but there is not so much as a modern paperback, nor yet a television set.

Outside the house, the earthy smell of boxwood mixes with the perfume of jasmine, giving a serene and mysterious quality to a garden that has long been in repose. In a scenario of *Sleeping Beauty* meets *Le Grand Meaulnes*, I have been there in the early evening, when the emerald green tree frogs known as *rainettes* begin their low pitched, rhythmic banter. The once trim hedges, now scraggly and over twenty feet high, obstruct all views of the property from the surrounding streets. Despite its central location in relation to the town, there is a pervading sense of social isolation emphasised by ever-closed shutters. Unkempt shrubs and climbers have completely covered some corners of the garden; engulfed by the bracken are two small dependencies that once would have had the charm of miniature cottages. In peering through the clouded and cracked glass panes of the doors and windows one can see what must have been the outhouse where the Latour-Marliac staff processed their fruits, nuts and vegetables, with all the old tools and jars littering the countertops and floor.

Stepping down from the house, in the middle of the garden, and just to the side of a now-towering umbrella pine and cedar, one finds the lily pond. It is long and rectangular with rounded corners, edged in brick with steps leading down into it at both ends, almost like an old lap pool. The mortar is too fissured to hold water now, but it retains enough rainwater to maintain a thick carpet of sphagnum moss and water lily pads, punctuated by bulrushes. It is intriguing to wonder what water lily variety Bory, Alida or Édgard Latour-Marliac or, indeed, the

Laydekers would have planted in their personal pond. A question that remains unanswered because these lilies haven't flowered in many decades for want of division and open water. Next to the pond two palm trees grow into the canopy of two red-leafed maples, the latter having outpaced the former and stolen their sunlight long ago. The lawn that fills the space around the pond is a knee-high meadow, the domain of crickets and hedgehogs. A dilapidated greenhouse sits half open to the elements a bit further on, with earthenware pots and other rudiments of the gardener strewn about. Across the little back lane that leads to the nursery and runs along the perimeter of the garden, just to the other side of the hedges, is the old kitchen garden, which tumbles down to one of the streams that feed the nearby River Lot. Now naturalised, Latour-Marliac's bamboos still thrive to make a dramatic statement along its banks.

The kitchen garden is relatively small by 19th century standards because the family would have had ample farming land and orchards to produce large quantities of top fruit and staple vegetables – any surplus would have been processed, distributed amongst the workers or sent to market.

The house, gardens and nursery welcomed visitors during the summer especially during July when the water lily flowers were at their zenith.

Above: Created in the 1990s, the modern lake covers some of the original culture ponds or bassins. Dervilly, writing in 1892, described this area as: 'The centre of aquatic exploitation occupies the two banks of a pretty stream whose mother-of-pearl waters gurgle gaily across a bed of pebbles; bamboos and shrubs grace the perimeters.'

Facing page: The red roses on the pergola are reflected nestling amongst the water lilies. The pergola provides a delightful view point over the *bassins*. In the early days Latour-Marliac ordered roses to sell as well as for his garden. They were one of the plants on which he swapped knowledge with the Comte de Castillon.

The Great Exhibitions Paris and Chicago

'The fun at the exhibition continues, and the Champ de Mars's atmosphere is more quicksilvery than ever. Nothing is finished yet, but the Eiffel Tower is open to the second platform. The public can go up there on foot, for the elevators cannot work before a fortnight. … There is no use in trying to epitomize the exhibition in routine, for it partakes of all the kaleidoscopic delight of every Parisian fete. One should be able to fly like a bird to every enticing necessity, and even then half the fun and wit would be lost.' Paris, 18th May, 1889, *The New York Times*

The 1889 *Exposition Universelle* was planned to celebrate master-pieces on a grand canvas radiating from the Eiffel Tower. It was a perfect venue for France to showcase its prestige in the Arts as well as to place her on the world stage as an industrially and technologically equipped nation. The Tower's design was not without its critics, not least the horticultural commentator, Alexandre Godefroy-Lebeuf, who was in the vanguard of protest against the harshness of Gustave Eiffel's design. Nevertheless, the Eiffel Tower rose majestically from the Champs de Mars, which were landscaped down to the banks of the River Seine, and across the water up to the fantastical buildings of the Trocadero. In all, the *Exposition* covered nearly a square kilometre.

Above: The view from under Gustave Eiffel's tower to the re-landscaped Trocadero Gardens where Latour-Marliac created his award winning exhibit. The Eiffel Tower received mixed reactions and was planned to be a temporary structure.

Facing page: The Trocadero Gardens today. 'The horticulture and arboriculture is centred in the gardens of the Trocadero, and it may be mentioned that it is intended to change all the flowering plants, which can bear change, once a fortnight'. (Guide to the Paris Exhibition, 1889)

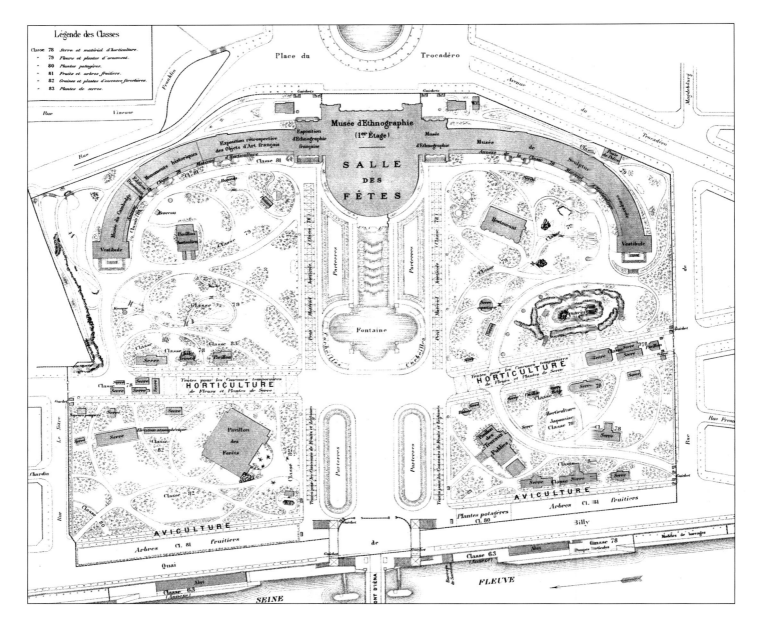

Plan of the Trocadero, *Exposition Universelle Internationale de 1889, Ministère du Commerce de l'Industrie et ses Colonies*. The exhibition brochure hailed: 'The engineer and the man of science will find there the latest discoveries of the human intellect.' Such men and women could explore no less than 23 exhibition sites designed into the landscape and there was a discrete area for the storage of empty cases.

The view from the Eiffel Tower running up the centre of the site to the Trocadero 'palace' can be seen on the previous page. Positioned on the banks of the River Seine, the water theme continued with a central pool and stepped cascade.

Latour-Marliac applied to enter Group IX (79) Flowers and ornamental plants; other categories included (78) Conservatories and horticultural apparatus; (80) Vegetables; (81) Fruit and fruit trees; (Seeds and saplings of forest trees); and (88) Plants for conservatories. All of equal interest to Latour-Marliac and Monet, more tantalising evidence for the possible meeting of these two men.

Latour-Marliac sent the list of water lilies for exhibition on 24th

March 1889. They would be despatched on two dates, 15th April and 15th September, thus ensuring a magnificent display of flowers from June to the close in October. He marked those raised from his own crossings with an asterisk which applied to all in the first 15th April group: *Nymphaea* odorata 'Exquisita' (illustrated overleaf), as the names implies an exquisite small carmine pink water lily, with red leaves introduced in 1880, but now uncommon. Brand new for the *Exposition*, the *N. odorata* 'Rosacea' with rose-pink to salmon yellow flowers that was later featured in *Revue Horticole* in 1891. Introduced in 1879, N. 'Odorata Sulphurea' (see pp.81), described as a 'classic' water lily, differing from 'Chromatella', in that it has mottled saffron yellow flowers on long red stems. The others, using Latour-Marliac's nomenclature, were '*N.o. pygmaea helvola, *N.o.p. purpurea, *N.o. marliacea albida, *N.o.m. carnea, *N.o.m. chromatella.'

For 15th September, he listed: '*Nymphaea marliacea rosea, N. alba, N. candida, N. caspary, N. odorata alba (minor), N.o. rubra, N. flava, N. tuberosa, N.pygmaea alba.'

Godefroy-Lebeuf took a professional interest in the gardens and nursery exhibits that were to be staged opposite the Eiffel Tower in the Trocadero gardens. The Moorish-meets-Neo-classical design of the Palais du Trocadero dated back to an earlier exhibition in 1878, it was finally dismantled in 1937 to be replaced by the Palais de Chaillot. (These are 'palaces' in the sense that they housed great spectacles for the public, not in the sense of former palatial dwellings.) A key figure in the genesis of the 1889 *Exposition Universelle*, Jean-Charles Alphonse Alphand was an engineer who had worked with Baron Haussman and redesigned many Parisian parks and squares. A speciality was the creation of dramatic cascades and water scenes. The statues of the Continents that can be seen today in front of the Musée d'Orsay were originally placed along the façade of the Palais du Trocadero.

Through the columns and illustrations in *Revue Horticole*, and the publication of '*Notice sur les Nymphaea & Nelumbium Rustiques – Leur culture et celle d'autres plantes aquatiques*', Godefroy-Lebeuf had helped establish Latour-Marliac as the specialist on water lilies. In June 1888, Latour-Marliac wrote to him confirming that he intended to exhibit nine water lilies, which included his most beautiful hybrids: *Nymphaea odorata rubra*, a subspecies with bright carmine flowers also known as the Cape Cod water lily, the large yellow-flowered *N.* 'Odorata Sulphurea', as well as *N.* 'Marliacea Chromatella' *N.* 'Caroliniana Nivea', with its magnificent 15cm-wide flowers, *N.* 'Marliacea Rosea' and *N.* 'Pygmaea Helvola'. However, Latour-Marliac expressed concern that the rules for his category, Classe 79 – Flowers and Ornamental Plants, and its associated costs would be prohibitive. (Monet and his fellow Impressionists expressed much the same sentiment about their part of the exhibition.)

In essence this would be the first time that the general public would have seen hardy coloured water lilies. In order to compete for the most beautiful display of *Plantes aquatiques de plein air*, Latour-Marliac would aim to have at least eight hybrid water lilies flowering from June to October. In the meantime, the usual exchange of articles and international magazines continued between Latour-Marliac and Godefroy-Lebeuf, including a chromolithograph of Latour-Marliac in January 1887. This placed him amongst other distinguished and erudite botanists. As a subscriber to *Revue Horticole*, one cannot help but wonder whether Monet might have seen any of these articles or engravings of the new Latour-Marliac water lilies?

On 15th March Latour-Marliac sent a parcel and note with advice on checking them out, and to be aware of the cold in Paris. He advised delaying planting them out until April. On 6th April confirmation was sent to the *Directeur General* that admission No. 19525 weighing 34 kilos had been despatched. The next day Latour-Marliac reconfirmed that the package was for Group IX Trocadero, *Classe 79*. He sent instructions directly to the Superintendant of the Trocadero, M Lefebvre, that the plants were arriving by *grand vitesse*. They would need to be potted up to their necks in the soil that he had supplied and then plunged into the little river of the Trocadero. The seventeen hardy water lilies were to be displayed with the strongest towards the centre and would be at their apogee from 12th to 29th July. Care and attention were paramount. He followed up on 8th April with further advice, another letter was sent to the Secretary to watch Lefebvre. Then Lefebvre informed him that nothing had arrived – where were they?

One can imagine Latour-Marliac's fury, as letters fly back and forth and a new package was sent. It transpired that the package had actually been awaiting collection from 6th April at the Gare d'Orléans. The Stationmaster at Villeneuve and Godefroy-Lebeuf were all approached to shed light on what went wrong. It was decided to return the original batch. However, far from being the anticipated disaster, the plants proved to be in remarkably good shape. This unexpected trial proved that *nymphaea* could survive several weeks in the post, thus opening up the possibility of marketing water lilies by train around Europe and by boat across the world.

All of his efforts were rewarded, as he won Premier Prix. In a long article commissioned for *The Garden* magazine in 1893, Latour-Marliac wrote:

'1889 rang in the *Exposition Universelle* in Paris, and [my] small collection of hybrids shyly took the road to the capital to solicit the attention of plant lovers in a setting of the world's earthly delights! There their good grace was appreciated and they returned radiant crowned by a first prize. What changes since that epoch, and how their countenance would have been even more daring if they had had amongst them the resplendence that has appeared amongst the new generation! …

The success obtained at the *Exposition Universelle* revived my spirit of competition and I harnessed myself once more to the task of attaining a hybridisation that was capable of procreating a vivid red far superior to those of the *N. Sphaerocarpa* and *N. odorata rubra*, both had been acknowledged as incapable of delivering this. After compelling trials and errors, I finally achieved my objective which was for the plant to display the same colours as the tropical Rubra and to be endowed with the inestimable property of seed bearing; a quality all the more important because it does not generate offsets.'

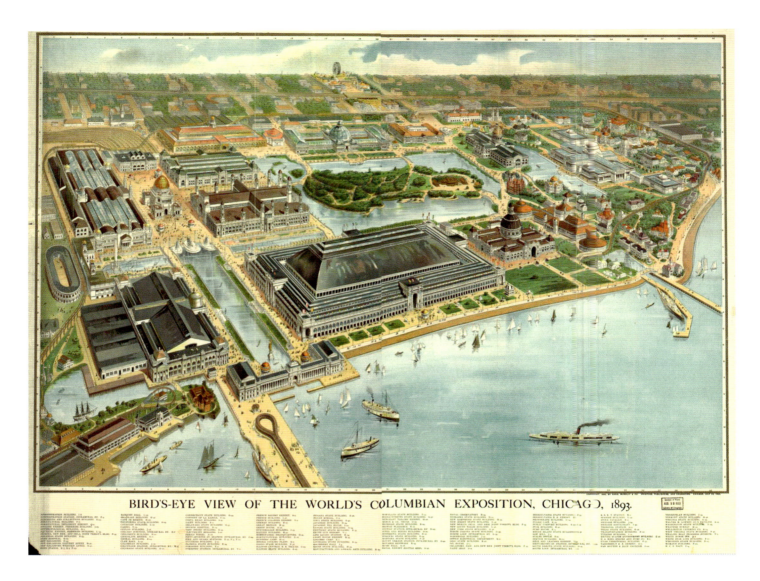

BIRD'S-EYE VIEW OF THE WORLD'S COLUMBIAN EXPOSITION, CHICAGO, 1893.

World's Columbian Exposition, Chicago 1892/93

'The Emerald City is built all of beautiful marbles in which are set a profusion of emeralds, everyone exquisitely cut and of very great size. There are other jewels used in the decorations inside the houses and palaces, such as rubies, diamonds, sapphires, amethysts and turquoises. But in the streets and upon the outside of the buildings only emeralds appear, from which circumstance the place is named the Emerald City of Oz. It has nine thousand, six hundred and fifty-four buildings, in which lived fifty-seven thousand three hundred and eighteen people, up to the time my story opens.'

The Emerald City of Oz, Frank L. Baum
(inspired by the World's Columbian Exposition)

The World's Columbian Exposition opened to the public on 1st May 1893 and over the following six months more than 27 million people explored the 600 acres (2.4 square kilometres). It was located in Jackson Park and on the Midway Plaisance in the Chicago districts of South Shore, Jackson Park Highlands, Hyde Park and Woodlawn.

The Exposition provided the genesis of the City Beautiful Movement and what became known as Olmstedian parks (after the landscape architect Frederick Olmsted) on a large scale as part of urban and suburban planning. Typically, central buildings had an axis onto shallow pools of water. In 1896 The Garden and Forest: a journal of Horticulture, landscape art and forestry reported on the legacy of Messrs. Olmsted:

' … in preparing all these attractions and conveniences the primary purpose of the park has never been lost sight of, the landscape is the essence of the park. The green pastures and still waters – pictures of peace – the outlook over the great inland sea all the commanding charm of the place, has been preserved and heightened for the refreshment of city-wearied senses.'

Above: Situated along the shores of Lake Michigan, the Exposition was open to the world to arrive by land or sea – 27 million visitors made the journey and were able to ride on the world's first Ferris Wheel.

Clockwise from top left:
Nymphaea 'Odorata Exquisita' was one of Latour-Marliac's earliest hybrids dating to around 1880.

Nymphaea 'Marliacea Albida'. A Latour-Marliac hybrid introduced in 1879. It was available for the 1893 *Exposition* and is possibly the white water lily on the Lincoln Park postcard (overleaf). In 1890 Latour-Marliac described it: … *has very large white flowers of 20cm (7⅞in) diameter, of which the exterior petals are pink-washed, … abundant and sustained flowering season from May to October.* Not only plants, Impressionist paintings were amongst the firsts at the *Exposition*, a founding trustee of Chicago's Art Institute, Martin A. Ryerson became an avid collector of Monet and finally visited him at Giverny in 1920. Despite generous offers, Monet refused to sell him his water lily panels.

Nymphaea odorata alba – a species varietal rather than a hybrid – was introduced from North America in 1789.

Nymphaea 'Odorata Sulphurea Grandiflora' was amongst the water lilies ordered for Chicago's Lincoln Park by its Superintendent, J.A. Pettigrew who had been in touch since 1891 in the build-up for the 1893 *Exposition*. Latour-Marliac promised to send plants the following April.

LILY POND IN LINCOLN PARK, CHICAGO

Left: Water lily pond at Lincoln Park, Chicago.

Below: Latour-Marliac used a shorthand for dates based on the Latin origin of the month names. So 2 7bre 1893 on this letter actually means 21st September 1893. Unfortunately due to the wrong address, Pettigrew's letter of 21st July had only arrived on 15th September, so the 2 each of N. odorata exquisita, o.sulphurea and pygmaea helvola plus one Laydekeri rosea could not be sent until the following April.

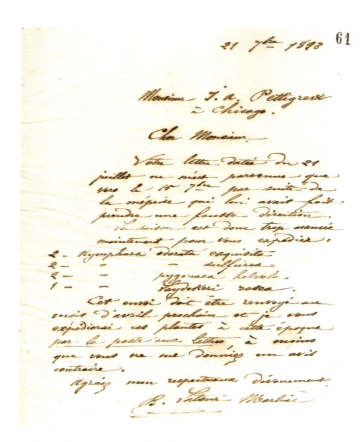

J.A. Pettigrew, the Superintendent of Lincoln Park, Chicago. Pettigrew transformed Chicago's Lincoln Park with water lilies of 'every kind he can obtain', including heating one basin with pipes for an exotic display. Just five years later when William Tricker published *The Water Garden*, he praised the parks of Chicago for being leaders in the fashion for aquatic gardening with an illustration of a pool in Union Park.

1900 *Exposition Universelle*, Paris

1900 – a new century in which dozens of dazzling new *nymphaea* would continue to be launched from their Templar source and a century in which they would find global sensation via Monet's new pond in Giverny where they were readily colonising. The *Exposition* was designed to look back and celebrate the achievements of the past century whilst looking forward to the future potential and developments of the 20th century. Paris' Grand Palais and Petit Palais were built for the occasion between 1897 and 1900, off the Champs-Elysée. The *Exposition* opened on 15th April and closed on 12th November 1900.

In the eleven years since Paris' last great exhibition, Latour-Marliac's stature as horticulturist had blossomed. In response to a request for advice from M Abel Chatenay on how best to organise displays for the forthcoming *Exposition*, he wrote:

'…With regard to the river that you propose to have flowing in view across the concourse, I think that it would sensible to give it a depth of at least 40 to 50 centimetres, be aware that if the tank is too deep it will not reheat sufficiently for water lilies that grow best in warm waters thus slowing their development; the width is of little importance and can be varied

By 1892 Latour-Marliac had built up a regular correspondence and exchange of water lilies with the American nurserymen and water lily breeders William Tricker, Edmund Sturtevant and L.W. Goodell as well as private customers. Although he did not create an exhibit as such, the vast Horticultural Hall and associated gardens provided a showcase for his hardy hybrids. Latour-Marliac had despatched *Nymphaea* in May 1891, the first of several orders, to

according to the whims of the architect and the needs of perspective; however, in total a minimum of 3 to 6 metres is preferable and when using rockwork the structure can be entirely arbitrary.

It seems to me that it will be very well placed between the two great palaces as well as servicing the aquatic plants in the four round *bassins*. I am not taking account of what the surface and depth of these *bassins* will be, but I am persuaded that this will be the best place for my *Nymphaea*.

As I have already described I will exhibit about forty *N.* hybrids which will need a water surface of around 60 to 100 square metres.'

Above: *Nymphaea* 'Pygmaea Helvola' – introduced by Latour-Marliac in 1879 as a result of crossing *N. pygmaea* and *N. mexicana*. It is small enough to be grown in a goldfish bowl. The miniature red *N.* 'Pygmaea Purpurea' is a varietal of tetragona introduced 1888.

Right: *Nymphaea* 'Marliacea Chromatella' was Latour-Marliac's first hybrid introduced in 1877. The large flowers are yellow and long blooming, whilst the leaves have characteristic deep chestnut brown mottled markings.

His letter carries on:

'It is worthwhile exhibiting two examples of each variety. I estimate therefore that there would be every advantage in massing them in the *bassins* adjacent to the palaces. All the examples that I will send are of French origin only and will be starting to flower immediately. *Voilà* the theory for the principal section of my exhibition. In part this should be the case for the Administration, saving that there may be too many entries, there will be a need for other plants to fill these water features, I would derive great pleasure in putting at your disposition about fifty very strong examples of my most beautiful hybrids, in 20 or 25 varieties, which could then be considered outside the concourse and which I would leave in place until the closing of the *Exposition*.

Also to add to the decorative charm of my exhibition I would set off my *N.* hybrids with 5 or 6 species of floating plants that would fill the spaces.

Finally I have obtained the seeds at Le Temple-sur-Lot, which are hardy outside all the year round here. I am firmly convinced, without making any promises that these splendid *Nymphaea* will flower more or less abundantly under the Paris sky…' .

Blue water lilies were an abiding fascination for Latour-Marliac (to breed hardiness into them would prove an unfulfilled dream), and later in August he wrote again to Abel Chatenay enclosing an article from *The Garden* corroborating his suggestions for having a display of blue and violet *Nymphaea* from his collection during the *Exposition*. Although they could not be put in place until June and realistically flowering would not really get underway until July, Latour-Marliac reckoned the continuing beauty through October and into November would be worth the delay. As a little sweetener Latour-Marliac enclosed some hardy perfumed flowers as a taste of what could be enjoyed from June onwards.

Latour-Marliac's health had suffered badly during the winter of 1899/1900, which prevented him travelling up to Paris in person. He was also approaching his 70th birthday. It did not stop him sending Chatenay his latest catalogue in February

Right: Latour-Marliac was ambitious to showcase his blue water lilies, although not hardy their scent and shimmering colour would provide a stunning display in front of the Petit Palais. This modern blue, *Nymphaea* 'Director George T. Moore' was introduced in 1941. The namesake was Director of the Missouri Botanical Garden in St. Louis from 1912 to 1953.

Below: *Nymphaea* 'Star of Zanzibar' introduced by Rich Sacher in 2000, a noted hybridiser of New Orleans. By 1900 Latour-Marliac had raised new varieties from *N. zanzibariensis* and offered six plants for the *Exposition*. Much to his disappointment they were refused.

with asterisks marking his new varieties, plus mention of the further twelve as yet unnamed, making a grand total of 40 French-bred hardy water lilies.

Despite the *bassins* of the Jardin du Petit Palais being larger than he expected, Latour-Marliac sent 24 varieties of hardy water lilies. In the package were three unnamed flowers of such exceptional merit that he hoped to give them grand names: President Loubet, Georges Leygues and Architecte Girault (who was responsible for planning the Grand Palais).

The original 24 *Nymphaea* were 'Andréana', 'Arc-en-Ciel', 'Atropurpurea', 'Aurora', 'Colossea', 'Eburnea', 'Ellisiana', 'Gloriosa', 'Laydekeri Floribunda', 'L. Fulgens', 'L. Lilacea', 'L. Purpurata', 'L. Punicea', 'Lucida', 'Marliacea Albida', 'M. Chromatella', 'M. Ignea', 'M. Rosea', 'M. Rubra Punctata', 'Odorata Sulphurea Grandiflora', 'Robinsonii', 'Sanguinea', 'Spectabilis', and 'Architecte Girault' … '(or Radiosa, if he declined the offer of giving it his name. Very large perfectly formed flower, lilac tinged carmine pink)'. All were chosen as the most repeat flowering.

On 1st July Latour-Marliac wrote once more to Édouard André regarding the *Exposition*, to confirm that he had exhibited 41 varieties, all of which were of French origin. The initial 24 had been supplemented by 'Caroliniana Nivea', 'Caroliniana Perfecta', 'Chrysantha', 'Formosa', 'Fulva', 'Gracillisma', 'Laydekeri Rosea', 'Marliacea Carnea', 'M. Flammea', 'Mosaïque', 'Odorata Exquisita', 'O. Sulphurea', 'Pygmaea Helvola', 'Seignoureti', 'Speciosa', 'Stella Alba', 'Suavissima' and 'Vésuve'. Further leaves of 'Arc-en-Ciel' and 'Mosaïque' were sent.

He had provided a show of importance throughout the summer. In an article later, André wrote a glowing report about the Latour-Marliac displays for which he was very grateful; however, his 'Concours d'Exposant' had been badly organised indeed 'pathetic' by comparison. As the *Exposition* was drawing to a close, good news was received from Mr R. Viger, the Deputy President of the *Société Nationale d'Horticulture de France*, Latour-Marliac had been nominated by the Minister of Agriculture to receive the award of *Chevalier du Merite d'Agricole*. One can imagine that the colour and scent of his water lilies must have offered respite from imports such as the talkies and diesel engines.

The Hardy Water Lily

'The acquisition of a red flowered hybrid Nymphaea which yields seed has opened up a new prospect by affording the means of effecting crossings with the yellow flowered kinds, the result being the production of quite a legion of Nymphaeas bearing flowers which exhibit singular shades of colouring, such as orange, vermilion, gold colour, etc.'.   B. Latour-Marliac

Today water lily gardeners grow the outcome of Latour-Marliac's life's work but how he achieved it has created theories as colourful as his hybrids.

The *Nymphaea* 'Marliacea Chromatella' was Latour-Marliac's first successful crossing of pollen from *N.* (*flava*) *mexicana* on to *N. alba* and it was introduced in 1877. The 'Marliac' prefix was used for all hybrids that had *N. alba* as the seed parent and species from the Castalia group. The Marliaceas were produced between 1877 and 1894. The 'Laykdekeri' group of varieties were bred between 1893 and 1900. Latour-Marliac achieved visually pleasing reds by intersubgeneric crosses between tropical and hardy water lilies. He revealed this in one of his letters to William Robinson:

> 'I have never wished to use the *N. Sphaerocarpa* (*N. Caspary* or *alba rubra*) for my artificial raisings, noting that they were neither sufficiently floriferous nor red in colour. I used to prefer *N. rubra des indes …*'

The successful progeny were often the outcome of a second generation and invariably sterile.

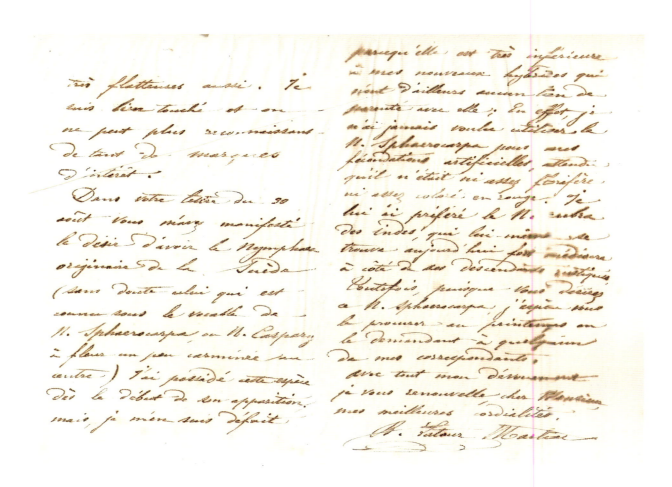

After 1900 neither Marliacea nor Laydekeri prefixes were used. The long lost N. 'Laydekeri Grandiflora' was also a result of the same cross – once more the difficulty is to decide

---

Previous spread: *Nymphaea* **'Cynthia Ann'** (2001, Strawn). Free flowering with coppery pink blossoms that are held above the water on long stems. Kirk Strawn visited Le Temple-sur-Lot several times in the 1990s. Large water lily, suitable for lakes and ponds.

Facing page: The second page of a letter to William Robinson, in which Latour-Marliac states that he preferred to use '... N. *rubra des indes* which in itself is found to be very mediocre alongside its hardy descendents'. (19th September, 1893)

Above: Loseley Park in Surrey, which is less than three miles from Jekyll's house and garden at Munstead Wood. Today it is happily colonised, albeit not colourfully, with water lilies.

whether he used the long-accepted N. *alba rubra* or N. *rubra des indes* to cross with N. *tetragona*? Either way, this progeny proved to be a highly fertile seed bearer and was just used for breeding (again safeguarding against his commercial water lilies self setting). In turn, it was crossed with *mexicana* pollen resulting in N. 'Robinsonii', 'Andréana', 'Aurora', 'Ellisiana', 'Fulva', 'Gloriosa', 'Sanguinea', 'Seignoureti' and 'Lucida'. *Nymphaea mexicana* pollen was also used on N. *tetragona* (aka N. *pygmaea* 'Alba') to produce N. 'Pygmaea Helvola'.

Many of Latour-Marliac's hybrids have the prefix *odorata* because he used that species as a seed parent, examples include: N. 'Odorata Exquisita', 'Luciana', 'Sulphurea' and 'Sulphurea Grandiflora'. The selected seedlings from N. 'Caroliniana' were indicated by the prefix Caroliniana as in N. 'Caroliniana Nivea', 'C. Perfecta' and 'C. Rosea'. Many of his final hybrids did not set viable seed, such as 'Amabilis'; it is generally accepted that he worked towards this outcome

PLAN OF A WATER LILY POND.

X, lake for Water Lilies (Nymphaeas) : 1 to 16, selected Nymphaeas. Y, islands, Salix Babylonica or other varieties of Weeping Willows on grass. Z, gravel path with rustic Oak branch bridge. A, grass. Plants on margin of lake : 1 to 18 ; trees and beds of shrubs on grass : 19 to 24.

Not all l y ponds were rectangular or round, Walter P. Wright, Horticultural Superintendent under the Kent County Council, included this design in his 1907 'Beautiful Gardens How to Make and Maintain Them'. Wright noted: 'Happily, the beautiful Water Lilies will thrive in much more circumscribed surroundings than those which they enjoy in the gardens of wealthy flower-lovers. The small pool in the home garden may have them. They will even enjoy life, and reward the grower, in tubs set in some cool spot, with the roots secure from hard winter frosts. … There is a splendid choice of hardy Nymphaeas among the Laydekeri, Marliacea, and other hybrids. Ellisiana may be noted as a good red, and James Brydon as a crimson. Laydekeri rosea is a charming pink. Marliacea albida, white and Marliacea chromatella, yellow, with marbled leaves, are two of the finest hybrids associated with the name of the famous raiser, Monsieur Latour-Marliac'.

in order to stop further experimentation with his hybrids. *

Over a century later the fact that his hybrids do not set seed has prevented their proliferation in many hues, in addition it has meant that they are still popular and true to their original colours. By readily setting seeds, many modern varieties have rapidly crossed themselves out of existence.

It goes without saying that the flowers would be the first selling point for the customer but a secondary consideration was the potential size of the plant depending on whether they had a lake, a small pool or a tub. The rhizomes provide a distinct indication for the breeder as to the cultivar and its size: the Marliacea were medium to vigorous with a distinct rhizome. Gertrude Jekyll, in *Wall and Water Gardens* (1901), described them as '… better suited to shallow water, say from

---

*The long-held belief that he was secretive about his crosses and methods has become something of an urban myth, repeated by his descendents and the garden press in general. In contrast, the tone of his letters indicate a willingness and pleasure in exchanges of knowledge with an enthusiasm for fellow botanists and gardeners to visit his grounds to witness his experiments. Could it be that his 'secrets' were only understood by his wife, son Edgard and a handful of contemporaries? After their deaths a confession of ignorance would not have been nearly so interesting as the idea of a scientific secret taken to the grave.

eighteen inches to two feet in depth. All are sweetly scented. These Nymphaeas are all quite recognisable by their peculiar, hard, wiry-looking root-stock, which is long and slender…' The Laydekeri are similar but recognisably smaller; the *odorata* species has a distinctive rhizome; the *tuberosa* is equally distinctive; and, as one would expect, the tiny 'Pygmaea Helvola' has very small rhizomes. As William Robinson wrote in *The English Garden*:

'But if neither ponds nor tanks are available these Water-Lilies can still be easily grown, for, as M. Latour-Marliac says, they can, like Diogenes, content themselves in a tub'.

The 19th-century taste for colour in the garden reached garish extremes, firstly in the grand parterres of the great and then in ambitious municipal carpet and seasonal bedding schemes. William Robinson, editor of *The Garden*, reviled such designs. A French chemist, Michel-Eugene Chevreul initiated the horticultural understanding of manipulating colour for maximum effect in his book *De la loi du contraste simultané des couleurs** (published in 1839, and translated

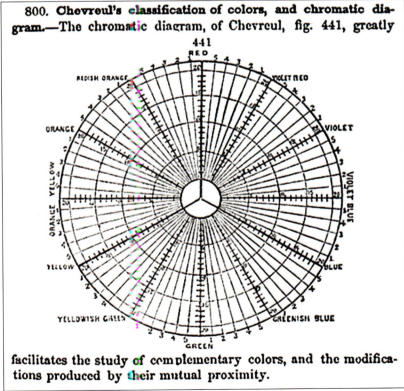

800. Chevreul's classification of colors, and chromatic diagram.—The chromatic diagram, of Chevreul, fig. 441, greatly

441

facilitates the study of complementary colors, and the modifications produced by their mutual proximity.

Above: Gertrude Jekyll's illustration of the margins of a pond with *Nymphaec odorata* in *Wall and Water Gardens* (1901). She provided a lengthy list of available water lilies at the back of the book, the selection for pink odoratas was as follows: '*Nymphaea odorata exquisita* is a charming form; it is a lovely shade of rosy-pink extending to the extremities of the petals. *Nymphaea odorata rosacea*, much paler in colour than the preceding, and quite as beautiful in its tints; a profuse flowering plant. *Nymphaea odorata suavissima*, another variety, the flowers of which are stated to be larger than the foregoing, but of the same tints, possibly darker on the whole. *Nymphaea odorata Luciana*, in the way of *N. odorata exquisita*, perhaps lighter in colour of the two'.

Left: Chevreul's Chromatic Diagram. The garish flower bedding schemes that adorned municipal parks across Europe were inspired by Michel-Eugene Chevreul's book on mixing and placing colours for maximum effect. As well as strictly geometric horticultural arrangements, artists such as Monet were also greatly influenced by his theories.

*It is a lengthy tome, with Part II, Division V, Sub-section I 'Application on the Law of Contrast of Colours to Horticulture' of key interest. Also of interest Chapter I 'On the Art of Arranging Ornamental Plants in Gardens, so as to derive the greatest possible advantage from the colours of their flowers' in which he extols the virtues of proportionate distribution of flower colours to create a unified sensation.

into English as *The Principles of Harmony and Contrast of Colours* in 1855). The effects of his arguments were interpreted to impressionistic effect by at least two of Latour-Marliac's customers: artist-gardener Claude Monet and gardener-artist Gertrude Jekyll.

Whether or not Latour-Marliac read the original book, its theories were expounded throughout gardening literature. They were colourfully displayed in the landscaping around the 1889 *Exposition Universelle*, the same year in which Chevreul died at the grand old age of 102.

Whatever the science behind plant colouring, the colour of water lilies is changeable. There are differences between the first two years of flowering and thereafter the variations in soil and water chemistry, as well as the time of day, will all have an effect. William Robinson had commissioned a long article from Latour-Marliac in 1893 for *The Garden* and these were the colourful subjects to which he drew the readers' attention:

> 'After numerous trials and experiments I at last succeeded in attaining the object of my desires in a hybrid, the flowers of which are of the same colour as those of the tropical *N. rubra*, … it has produced seedlings the flowers of which exhibited a whole scale of intermediate shades of colour, from soft pink to the deepest red. …'

In 1899, Latour-Marliac described as his favourite water lilies:

> The creamy-yellow-pink of *N.* 'Chrysantha',
> The whites of 'Colossea' and 'Eburnea',
> The carmine of 'Froebeli',
> The pinks of 'Laydekeri Punicea', 'Odorata Speciosa',
>   'Odorata Suavissima', 'Panorama',
> The deep dark red of 'Odorata Atropurpurea'.

One of Gertrude Jekyll's laments was the inability of nurserymen to correctly and accurately describe the colours of their plants. When she discovered Latour-Marliac's water lilies and later corresponded with him, I hope her heart rejoiced at the nuances of colour he encapsulated when christening them.

Although it is simplistic, the easiest way to explore Latour-Marliac's water lily legacy is by separating their colours into the horticultural categories of white, yellow, red, pink and copper that can still be seen on his ponds at Le Temple-sur-Lot. Most described in this chapter are of his breeding but all are rooted in his inspiration. Breeding hardiness from the tropical blue water lily of legend eluded him and other hybridisers for a century. This story is placed separately at the end of the chapter.

Tranquility at Le Temple-sur-Lot. 'A lake is the landscape's most beautiful and expressive feature. It is the earth's eye looking into which the beholder measures the depth of his own nature' Thoreau.

White

Asleep upon the stream,
The moonlight stream,
The water lilies dream –
Floating they dream.
With cups of purest white
All folded from the night.'
                    Quoted by Mrs C.F. Leyel in *Compassionate Herbs*, 1946

White is where it all starts for Latour-Marliac and his quest to introduce hardy colours into the common white water lilies of three continents. However, he also hybridised whites into elaborate shapes with subtle variations.

The botanical specific names following the genus are usually of Latin origin, *alba* being the obvious signifier of white. In his 1972 guide to nomenclature, William Stearn lists no less than 14 compounds such as *albiflorus* for white flowered, *albiplenus* for double white flowers, *albicans* for off-white and *albida* for whitish. One European native is the robust, small but fully petticoated *N.* 'Alba Plenissima'. *N. candida* is the hardiest Northern European and Northern Asian water lily. A North American native, the white *N. odorata*, was named by William Aiton in 1789, it is more commonly known as the Fragrant Water Lily or Beaver Root but it can be a thug in the Great Lakes region. One further white parent is from China – the *N. tetragona*.

Latour-Marliac's earliest hybrid whites were both introduced in 1880: *N.* 'Hermine', with star-shaped flowers and long, pointed petals; and *N.* 'Marliacea Albida' which despite its unexciting 'whitish' sobriquet, has a mass of milky white pointed petals with lightly pink tinted outer petals that can attain a diameter of 20cm (7¾in). The bright snow white *N.* 'Caroliniana Nivea' was introduced in 1893, with the added bonus of large flowers with fine wispy petals. In 1907 *N.* 'Lactea' was introduced, followed a year later by 'Virginalis' whose large 15cm (6in) flowers are cup shaped, slightly fragrant and creamy milk purest white; it proved very successful for Latour-Marliac. In 1910, enter the *N.* 'Albatros' with large snow-white flowers and a yellow heart and later *N.* 'Gonnère',* which also has snow-white flowers but larger, double and with a mass of yellow pollen holding anthers.

Stocks have been built up again of the 1901 introduction *N.* 'Arc-en-Ciel', the rainbow of its name runs across the leaves rather than the pinky-white flowers. Mrs Richmond, the author of *In My Lady's Garden*, gave a perfectly evocative description:

'a plant which is distinguished from all others by the extraordinary beauty of its leaves, which are tinted when they first unfurl on the water with brilliant carmine, apricot, and crimson, like those of *Ampeolopsis veitchii* in autumn, making a delightful contrast to the creamy pink blossoms'

In the States, George Richardson, whose nursery was based at Warren, Trumbull County, Ohio, introduced a number of white water lilies, all of which interested Latour-Marliac: first *N.* 'Tuberosa Maxima' in 1880; 'Tuberosa Richardsonii' in 1894; then in 897 a form of *alba*, *N.* 'Gladstoniana', with white star-shaped flowers; and later he also introduced the tropical *N. gigantea* 'Hudsoniana'.

In 1940, both Établissements Latour-Marliac and Miller Water Gardens of San Gabriel, California produced further whites. From Latour-Marliac, 'Elisée' (Elysée), a good classic white that was part of a WWII patriotic series. Miller's 'Hal Miller' is a cross between 'Virginalis' and 'Sunrise'; happy in semi-shade, the creamy white flowers have yellow inner petals that appear to reflect the saffron colour of the stamens, set against purple-blotched green pads.

Names such as Slocum, Stebor and Strawn are attached to post-war introductions. Perry D. Slocum (1913-2004), founder of Slocum Water Gardens and Perry's Water Gardens in North Carolina, was one of the most important breeders of aquatic plants. He held US patents for several lotuses and hardy water lilies and in 1986 the International Water Lily Society presented him with the Water Lily Hall of Fame Award. Two of his most successful whites are: 'Perry's White Wonder' (1990) and 'Venus' (1991). The former has white flowers and sepals with reddish undersides to the pads, while the latter has fragrant flowers that are blushed very pale pink, green tipped sepals and pads that are burgundy red whilst the upper surface has a wide green mid-stripe.

Dr Robert 'Kirk' Strawn (1922-2008) and his wife Charlene collected water lilies from growers across the world for their nursery Strawn Water Gardens. Until his retirement in 1991, Strawn was a lecturer at the Texas A&M University and is arguably the only breeder to come close to Latour-Marliac's work. He was a Founding Member of the International Water Lily Society and stood as its second president in 1991. As a result of his hybridisation programmes, he created 57 new cultivars. In 1991 and 1996 he visited the Établissements Latour-Marliac during the Davies' tenure, a year later he introduced the creamy white 'Denver'.

The Davies' legacy of a sinuous lake on which swans glide in Le Temple-sur-Lot is echoed in *N.* 'Lac des Cygnes', introduced by Robert Sheldon in 2009. As a finale, this 'Swan Lake' has golden stamens and the centre of the flower rises like a ballerina in a brilliantly white tutu.

---

*Although introduced in 1914, Nymphaea 'Gonnère' was undoubtedly one of Latour-Marliac's hybrids when the nursery was being run by his widow, Alida (née Gonnère) and their son, Édgard.

Nymphaea 'Caroliniana Nivea' (1893, Latour-Marliac). In 1899 Latour-Marliac recommended its 15cm distinguished flowers for Jeremiah Colman's fountain basin – presumably well away from the spray. Large and vigorous, suitable for lakes and ponds.

Nymphaea '**Hermine**' (1880, Latour-Marliac). One of Bory Latour-Marliac's earliest white hybrids with large flowers lasting from May to September. Medium-sized water lily, suitable for ponds and pools.

Nymphaea '**Alba Plenissima**'. A European native, this is a particularly free-flowering variant of *alba* with a double white cup set against green pads. Peak flowering is from July to September. Medium-sized water lily, suitable for ponds and pools.

Nymphaea 'Alba Delicata' (1899, F Henkel). Friedrich Henkel was an important German *nymphaea* specialist. This lily was re-introduced in 1912 by Lagrange. Spreading to cover a square metre of surface in 1-2 years. Medium-sized water lily; suitable for ponds and pools.

Above: *Nymphaea* 'White Sultan' (1991, Strawn). A good complement to colourful water lilies, it flowers abundantly and has a slight fragrance. Medium-sized water lily, suitable for medium-sized ponds. Amongst the 57 new cultivars created by Kirk Strawn, he listed 'White Sultan' as one of his lifetime favourites, along with Latour-Marliac's yellow N. 'Marliacea Chromatella'

Left top: *Nymphaea* 'Gladstoniana' (1897, Richardson). The work of American nurseryman George Richardson was of mutual interest to Latour-Marliac. His 1897 introduction boasts very big flowers, 14cm (5½in). Large water lily, suitable for large ponds and lakes.

Left centre: *Nymphaea* 'Venus' (1991, Slocum). Suitably star shaped flowers, fragrant and on long stems, and can be planted at depths of 40-100cm (15¾-39½in). They will cover a square metre within 1-2 years and are ideal for medium to large ponds. Perry D. Slocum (1913-2004) held US patents for several lotuses and hardy water lilies. This and 'Perry's White Wonder' (1990) are his most successful whites

> Those virgin lilies all the night,
> Bathing their beauties in the lake,
> That they may rise more fresh and bright,
> When their beloved sun's awake.
> Thomas Moore (1779-1852)

Left: *Nymphaea* 'Virginalis' (1907, Latour-Marliac). It has milky-white petals with stamens the colour of Cornish clotted cream, the flowers set in pale green pads. In 1913 it was awarded a Certificate of Merit. Large water lily, suitable for lakes and big ponds.

Nymphaea odorata is the white water lily native to North America. The N. *odorata rubra* is a natural mutation that was found in a kettle pond or Cape Cod. This hardy water lily is suitable for naturalising in medium sized ponds.

Nymphaea 'Lac des Cygnes' (1992, Latour-Marliac). An unnamed variety that was finally introduced and christened by Robert Sheldon in 2009. Medium-sized but vigorous, the unique form of its 10cm (4in) blossoms gently rise above the water surface and enjoy a sustained flowering period.

Nymphaea candida, one of the hardiest water lilies, its specific name *candida* means shining white and is also used in the naming of the Madonna lily, *Lilium candidum*. A small classic species from Eastern Europe and Eurasia, flowering in July and August. Small water lily that can be grown in a half-barrel or small pool.

Above: *Nymphaea* 'Marliacea Albida' (c.1880, Latour-Marliac). Described by Latour-Marliac as having 'very large white flowers of 20cm (7⅞in) diameter, of which the exterior petals are pink-washed.' Large water lily with an abundant and sustained flowering season from May to October and is suitable for naturalising on lakes.

Right: *Nymphaea* 'Arc-en-Ciel' (1900, Latour-Marliac). The rainbow in the name relates to the striations across the pads rather than the pink-tinged white flowers. Large water lily, suitable for naturalising on lakes.

Below: *Nymphaea* 'Tuberosa Richardsoni' (1894, Richardson). The *N. tuberosa* is a native of NE USA, the flowers are up to 23cm (9in) wide, pure white and slightly scented. Latour-Marliac ordered this water lily from America via William Robinson. Large water lily, suitable for lakes and ponds.

Overleaf: *Nymphaea* 'Hal Miller' (1940, Miller). Miller Water Gardens of San Gabriel, California was as well known for its goldfish varieties as water lilies. The founder was Hal Miller for whom this water lily is named, following the successful hybridisation of a 'Sunrise' with a 'Virginalis'. The flowers which look like a cactus dahlia can reach more than 30cm (12in) in diameter. Very large water lily, suitable for lakes and ponds.

Yellow

' I keep always a few of the fairest flowers, and call
this table the shrine. Sometimes it is a spray of
Madonna Lilies in a long white vase of ground glass,
or beneath the picture in a jar of yellow glass floats a
saffron-tinted Water Lily, the Chromatella, or a tall
sapphire glass holds deep blue Larkspurs of the same
shade... The lovely combinations and contrasts of
flowers and vases are simply endless'

Celia Thaxter, *An Island Garden*, 1894

Celia Thaxter's island garden was on Appledore, off the
coast of New England and during the summers she entertained
a panoply of guests filling her rooms with flowers, music and
food. She acted as muse to the Impressionist artist, Childe
Hassam, who illustrated *An Island Garden* and painted
Thaxter's gardens and interiors. She protected her water lilies
over winter by keeping them in barrels in her cellar.

Despite its name, the hardy European yellow pond lily is
not a *Nymphaea* i.e. a water lily. However its form inspired
the carvings of 13th century sculptors of the roof bosses in
great churches such as Westminster Abbey, Bristol Cathedral
and the Angel Choir at Lincoln Cathedral.

The manner in which they are crafted is perfectly
described by Geoffrey Grigson in the *Englishman's Flora* as
'where the sculptor gave a ripple and liquid sinuosity to the
leaves.' Grigson also notes that one of its common names,
'Brandy Bottle', is because the flowers smell of brandy dregs.

The horticultural definition of the colour yellow ranges into
shades of orange/peach/apricot, red and autumnal copper.
The canary yellow flowers of the tropical *N. mexicana* originate
in Mexico and Florida, as the names suggest, where they can
be invasive, so best for use as a parent rather than for ornament.
In 1877 Latour-Marliac created his first successful and still most
popular hybridisation, *N. 'Marliacea Chromatella'*.

In 1887 Latour-Marliac described the *N. 'Marliacea
Chromatella'* to George Nicholson of Kew as being the result
of thousands of annual sowings until he was satisfied that he
had obtained a strain of high interest with full flowers and
good foliage. It has also been called 'Yellow Marliac'.
Around the turn of the twentieth century in Australia, the
Botanical Gardens in Adelaide produced a more understated
yellow form of the 'Chromatella', which they named *N.
'Moorei'* for Charles Moore, the director of the Sydney
Botanic Garden from 1848-1896.

In 1879 Latour-Marliac introduced another highly
successful yellow, the star-shaped *N. 'Odorata Sulphurea'*.
The reader may have noticed in the archive illustrations that
Latour-Marliac spells 'Sulfurea' with an 'f', however, the
modern spelling is 'Sulphurea'. In 1888 he topped this with
the resplendent *N. 'Odorata Sulphurea Grandiflora'* sporting
larger flowers with longer petals. Twenty years later it was still

a top choice for Mrs Richmond 'the finest of the yellow
variety, the petals shading from pale primrose on the outer
edge to rich golden yellow in the centre, the foliage being
blotched with crimson-brown'. The smaller abundantly
floriferous canary yellow miniature *N. 'Pygmaea Helvola'*
was named in time for the 1889 *Exposition Universelle*.

New yellows as such do not feature again but autumnal
tints of yellow, orange and copper appear in three Latour-
Marliac varieties: the 1894 *N. 'Fulva'*, 1895 *N. 'Aurora'*,
and after his death the 1912 floriferous *N. 'Indiana'*. *N.
'Aurora'* was described by Mrs Richmond in 1908:

'the flowers opening in pale apricot, which is daily
more heavily flushed with carmine until the flower
closes. The blossoms of this lovely flower are not very
large, but can scarcely be surpassed in richness and
delicacy of tint'.

N. 'Colonel A.J. Welch' is attributed as a Latour-Marliac
hybrid, its date of introduction is given as 1929. The flower
stands proudly out of the water with immaculately tunic shaped
canary yellow petals, albeit with an excess of leaves. It is
viviparous i.e. bearing living young, and when new plants are
formed they remain anchored to the mother plant whilst they put
down long roots. As 'Colonel A.J. Welch' can grow in very
deep lakes or even moving water, it may well be two years
before the linking stems finally fall away. If the roots are not
securely established, the plants have to find a shallower home
where they can anchor and set up a new colony.

There are two modern Latour-Marliac yellows: the 1993
'David', a very pale apricot with egg yolk centre that is also
known as 'Orange Comanche'; and the 2003 'Yellow Enigma'.

Strawn named his first successful hybrid, the delicate
yellow 'Charlene Strawn,' for his wife. It is a hybrid of *N.
mexicana* and *N. odorata* that was introduced in 1987. This
was followed by the bright, free flowering 'Joey Tomocik' in
1993, and double flowering 'Lemon Chiffon' in 1999. The
extraordinary luminescent double creamy-yellow flowers of
'Innerlight' rise from a Marliac rhizome, it was introduced by
Strawn in 1997 and is fragrant.

Slocum achieved three new yellows in 1991: 'Gold Medal',
'Yellow Queen' and 'Yellow Sensation'. One further modern
yellow that features in today's Latour-Marliac catalogue is 'Texas
Dawn' (1990, Landon).

Facing page: *Nymphaea* 'Sulphurea Okeechobee' (1999, Florida
Aquatic Nurseries). Florida's Lake Okeechobee is one of the few places
where both *N. mexicana* and *N. odorata* grow together in nature.
Although this large cultivar is the result of a natural cross, sulphurea
acknowledges Latour-Marliac's legacy of the first hardy yellow.

Nymphaea 'Odorata Sulphurea Grandiflora' (1888, Latour-Marliac). One of the first water lilies ordered by Monet and later exhibited in 1900 by Latour-Marliac next to both the Grand and Petit Palais in Paris. Large water lily with double flowers with longer petals. Suitable for ponds and small lakes.

Facing page, top: *Nymphaea* 'Marliacea Chromatella' (1877, Latour-Marliac). Also known as 'Yellow Marliac', this was Latour-Marliac's first successful hybridisation. Floriferous from May to October. Hardy large water lily, suitable for naturalising on lakes.

Facing page, bottom: *Nymphaea* 'Pygmaea Helvola' (1879, Latour-Marliac). This abundantly floriferous miniature was exhibited by Latour-Marliac at the 1889 *Exposition Universelle*. It develops into a canary yellow hue and can be raised in a goldfish bowl or any small receptacle of 5 litres, under 10-20cm (4-7⅞in) of water.

Nymphaea mexicana. First recorded in 1832, it's a native of Florida and Mexico and is also known as the Banana Water lily. Although very attractive, its prolific growth can sometimes make it a nuisance.

Facing page: *Nymphaea* 'Odorata Sulphurea' (1879, Latour-Marliac). The stout reddish stem that rises clear above the water surface by up to 10-12cm (4-4¾in) and the pink undersides to the sepals of the star-shaped flowers make for easy identification. Saffron stamens and leaves mottled with chestnut complete the picture. This was one of Latour-Marliac's most successful yellows. Medium-sized water lily, suitable for pools and small ponds.

Copper

'Chrysantha, one of the most elegant varieties whose flowers start with a beautiful creamy pink that matures into a copper yellow, marbled brown leaves; golden-orange stamens'. B. Latour-Marliac 1899

Copper is possibly the hardest colour to define but Latour-Marliac's description above, for one of his favourites for shallow, small pools, N. 'Chrysantha' is as good as it gets. It has rounded petals that open in what today is described as a delicate shade of peaches-and-cream deepening to copper as it ages. The waxy lily pads are mottled. It was preceded in 1904 by N. 'Graziella', a small variety that is also good for small pools and containers. Its coppery yellow flowers evolve in different tones like 'Chrysantha' but less floriferously. The shot silk copper pink N. 'Seignoureti' with its egg yolk centre, which Latour-Marliac named for the statesman Seignouret was introduced in 1893. A century later it was almost lost to cultivation but recently stocks have been built up to good levels.

Three further hybrids exhibit Latour-Marliac's success in achieving copper-toned water lilies whose colours change as they age. The first was introduced in 1905 and named 'Paul Hariot' for the botanical artist, it has orange yellow flowers that deepen towards red during the second and third days of flowering. American Indian tribes seem to have been on his mind with the introduction of 'Comanche' and 'Sioux' in 1908. The compact, cup-shaped 'Comanche' opens with a pure coppery flower gradually softening to a deep apricot heart, this changes on the second and third days towards the final hues of copper red. 'Sioux' opens initially with light coppery yellow flowers with bronze-tinted interior petals, as the days pass they move through orange to a ruddy copper.

In 1929 Jean Laydeker introduced 'J.C.N. Forestier', which is an apricot to coppery orange colour on tall stems with green leaves speckled with purplish brown.

One of the last of the coppers out of the Latour-Marliac stable appeared in 1993 with the thoroughly modern name of 'Pam Bennett'. The Davies named this water lily for the wife of Norman H. Bennett who founded his aquatics nursery in 1959 ably assisted by Pam. They bought all their initial stocks of water lilies from Latour-Marliac. At Bennett's nursery he planted his swimming pool with N. 'Pam Bennett' accompanied by 60 golden orfe. Family lore recounts that his aunt embroidered water lilies on his christening robe. Closely resembling the copper 'Paul Hariot', its pale shades of yellow evolve to a light red.

Today Latour-Marliac stocks 'Karleen Harder' (1984, Harder) with 12cm (4¾in) flowers that are as large as the pads, accurately described as the most coppery of copper colours. The light coppery flowers of 'Peach Sunrise' are one of the largest at 14cm (5½in) diameter but matched by the luminous coppery double blooms of 'Carolina Sunset' (1991, Slocum). Larger still are the 15cm (6in) rounded double flowers of 'Florida Sunset' (1995, Slocum), which display a light copper shade with subtle hues of pink and, like the water lilies of mythology, the flowers rise graciously out of the water.

Strawn introduced many copper varieties, two of which are named for the former co-owner of Latour-Marliac: 'Barbara Davies' (1992) has 15cm (6in) almost double flowers of a uniform pale copper against lightly mottled pads. It is both vigorous and a profuse bloomer. He used her maiden name for the profusely blooming 'Barbara Dobbins' (1996), which also has 15cm (6in) flowers in coppery tones of pink and yellow that rise out of the water. 'Berit Strawn' (1993) is uncommon with compact, crinkled copper-pink coloured flowers around egg-yolk yellow stamens. 'Little Sue' (1993) rises like a star from the water against dark green shiny pads, whilst 'Patio Joe' (1997) apart from a long stem and large size, is similar to 'Little Sue'. 'Starbright' (1997) has pale copper petals that look as though they are in freefall. The almost double flowers of 'Sunny Fink' (1997) deepen to copper at its centre. Finally, on the Official Checklist of Water Gardeners International, Strawn is credited for the introduction of N. 'Thomas O'Brien' in 2005. It has 10cm (4in) star-shaped flowers that are fragrant and a copper-toned pink.

Facing page: *Nymphaea* 'Starbright' (1997, Strawn). The pale copper petals are very similar to those found on tropical water lilies. The dark green pads provide a good contrasting background. Medium-sized water lily, suitable for pools.

Overleaf: *Nymphaea* 'Seignoureti' (1893, Latour-Marliac). Latour-Marliac described the flowers as 'yellow, flamed with carmine, flushed with the pale pink of dawn'. The highly fertile seed bearing N. 'Laydeker Grandiflora' was crossed with pollen from N. *mexicana* to produce N. 'Seignoureti' as well as 'Robinsoni', and 'Ellisiana'. Small water lily, suitable for pools and containers.

Left: *Nymphaea* 'Barbara Davies' (1991, Strawn). The 15cm (6in) almost double flowers whose coppery tones are just discernible in full sunshine. Barbara Davies was co-proprietor of Établissements Latour-Marliac from 1991 to 2007 and is unusual in having two water lilies named for her. A large water lily suitable for pools and ponds

Below: *Nymphaea* 'Berit Strawn' (1993, Strawn). This rare compact almost luminescent water lily was obtained by crossing 'Rembrandt' with *mexicana*. The flowers are almost crinkled. A small jewel for miniature water gardens or a tub.

Facing page: *Nymphaea* 'Solfatare' (1906, Latour-Marliac). The pale almost pink creamy yellow matures into an intense orange bordering on red. Seemingly volcanoes fired Latour-Marliac's imagination in 1906 as it is the same year he introduced 'La Vésuve'. Excellent for small garden ponds and miniature aquatic gardens.

Nymphaea 'Chrysantha' (c.1899, Latour-Marliac). One of Latour-Marliac's favourite
water lilies for small pools. He launched it at the 1900 *Exposition Universelle* in Paris.

Facing page: *Nymphaea* 'Florida Sunset' (1995, Slocum). A large
vigorous water lily whose coppery tones run from light yellow to
pink blushed with pink. The long stems supporting double flowers
stretch elegantly above the water. Suitable for pools and lakes.

Nymphaea 'David' (1993, Latour-Marliac). Introduced by Ray and Barbara Davies during their tenure. The unusual orange-pink flowers darken as they age. Free flowering from June to September. Small water lily, suitable for pools and ponds in full sun.

Right: *Nymphaea* 'Thomas O'Brien' (2005, Strawn). The fragrant double pink-peachy copper flowers blossom freely from June through to late September. Best planted straight into clay soil, not suitable for growing in pots or baskets. Medium-sized water lily, suitable for naturalising in pools and ponds. The original Mr O'Brien after whom this is named co-owns the Flower Barn in Cambria County's Johnstown in Pennsylvania with George Griffith. In the 1940s the young George was encouraged by his uncle to sell the fragrant water lilies he had been raising, and ultimately the proceeds from his water plant and fish sales paid for his studies in horticulture at Penn State University. While a student, his talents were recognised in 1955 by the then president of Penn State, Milton Eisenhower, who wanted to celebrate his presidential brother Dwight's visit to the University. Griffith successfully transformed the pond in front of Milton's home by floating 2,000 water lilies across it, a feat that made the pages of *Life* magazine. He has since spent 50 years hybridising water lilies.

   Griffith has also been a guardian angel to a Manchurian variety of Chinese lotus (*Nelumbo nucifera*) that was raised from three ancient lotus seeds believed to be 2-3,000 years old, which were found in the muddy depths of a Manchurian lake in 1951. They were originally presented to Paul Souder working at the Kenilworth Aquatic Gardens, who managed to germinate them. With a view to increasing their chances of survival (and satisfying his curiosity) Griffith asked for and received a division. The Manchurian lotus flourished and bloomed for him at Johnstown and at his summer house in Ligonier.

Red

The 'reds' range from those associated with danger, the seeds of the pomegranate and vermilion through crimson, carmine, amaranth and lilac purple verging towards dark pink. The birthplace of Latour-Marliac is celebrated in one of the last hybrids to be introduced by his direct descendents in 1972, 'Château Le Rouge'. It is described as a superb, floriferous, small water lily whose pomegranate-red petals form symmetrical flowers. The eponymous château still stands in the nearby small town of Granges-sur-Lot. Three years earlier the name for the parcel of land on which the nursery sits was used for the new pomegranate-red 'Bateau'.

The 1889 'Marliacea Rubra Punctata' has red magenta flowers mixed with carmine around red-orange stamens. It is easy to grow and very floriferous. In 1890 'Laydekeri Purpurea' was described by Latour-Marliac as: 'magnificent variety, flowering non-stop from May to October with red and amaranth flowers; stamens orange red'.

The 1893 'Laydekeri Fulgens' has attractive deep pink flowers that deepen into a rich burgundy. Latour-Marliac described the new 'Marliacea Ignea' and 'Marliacea Flammea' as being 'without rival' in a letter to William Robinson on 4th March 1894. The latter has purple red flowers with a hint of white at their tips, the stamens are deep red and the leaves are brown marbled. By 1895 the vermilion red 'Robinsonii' was named in honour of William Robinson who had done so much to establish and encourage the growth of hardy coloured water lilies in both Great Britain and the USA. In Latour-Marliac's own words:

'The acquisition of a red flowered hybrid Nymphaea which yields seed has opened up a new prospect by affording the means of effecting crossings with the yellow flowered kinds …. The first of them which flowered being named after the editor of THE GARDEN, a compliment due to him in return for the great interest which he has taken in the advancement of the culture of hardy Nymphaeas.'

The long flowering raspberry red 'Andréana' was offered at the same time. 'Sanguinea' was introduced in 1894; as the name suggests, the flowers are a deep blood red.

The name 'Gloriosa' with its associations with the beautiful exotic scarlet blooms of the climbing Glory Lily, instantly conjures up a picture of vivid red and this 1896 introduction was described as a triumph – the glorious flowers are double, the outer tips are tinted with pale pink and scented. According to Mrs Richmond it was:

'a large and very handsome water-lily, about 8 inches across, in rich glowing crimson, with a copper-red central tuft of stamens adding greatly to its beauty'.

Such was their popularity that both 'Gloriosa ' and 'Andréana' were out of stock by 1907.

Named for his loyal English customer, Charles Ellis, 'Ellisiana' was introduced in 1896. Still in great demand, it has pomegranate-red flowers with lively orange stamens and is suitable for smaller *bassins*. Henry A. Dreer in Philadelphia became a frequent customer and also undertook his own crosses, one of which is the very popular 'James Brydon', introduced in 1899. The goblet-shaped flowers are double in a deep fuchsia, set against purple leaves that darken with age. Another Dreer introduction of 1902 is the pinky red 'Arethusa'. In 1901, Latour-Marliac introduced the Atropurpurea, which according to Mrs Richmond was:

'even darker in tint, with bronze foliage; but the blossoms are not quite so large as those of Gloriosa'.

In 1898 Swiss botanist Otto Froebel (1844-1906) introduced a blood-red water lily with olive green, distinctively spade-shaped leaves, which he named 'Froebeli'.

The brilliant red water lily 'La Vésuve' was introduced in 1906. The 1909 'Escarboucle' is a personal favourite for its French name which sounds far less exotic in English – carbuncle – and for its colour. It is a deep pinky-red, with large pomegranate-coloured petals striated with crimson sepals. 'Livingstone' is red with white striations as well as being fragrant. The same year, 'Meteor' with magenta red flowers striated with white appeared along with the ruby globe flowers of 'Splendida'. Unusually, as Latour-Marliac's hybrids are mostly sterile, Slocum used 'Splendida' several times as a parent for his new hybrids. Amongst nine novelties, three new reds were advertised in 1910: 'Attraction', 'Conqueror' and 'Sultan'; the first two are similar except that the latter is paler but with a crimson heart whilst 'Sultan' has large beautiful deep pink flowers and orange stamens. True to its name, the 1910 'Attraction' has very large flowers sometimes attaining a diameter of 25cm (9¾in). The magenta flowers contrast strikingly with the almost white sepals. Their size is matched by the vermilion flowers of the long-lasting 'Charles de Meurville' introduced by Latour-Marliac's grandson, Jean Laydeker, in 1931. After his father's death in 1911, Édgard Latour-Marliac introduced the large bright red flowered 'Sirius' in 1913, which is notable for its dark red mottled pads.

In 1927 'Maurice Laydeker' was introduced with crimson flowers striated with white and followed in 1936 by 'Madame Maurice Laydeker' whose round-shaped flowers display dark red on a white base. The magenta red 'Jean de la Marsalle' was also introduced that year, followed in 1965 by Jean Laydeker's remembrance of his work in Africa, the magenta red 'Senegal'. Whether it is a red sky in the morning or at night, the last Latour-Marliac deep red celebrates the nursery's location: 'Temple Fire', it was introduced by the Davies in 1993.

Facing page: *Nymphaea* 'Bateau' (1969, Latour-Marliac). This was one of the last to be introduced by the Laydeker descendents in 1969; like 'Chateau le Rouge' it is likely to be a reinvention of 'Laydekeri Fulgens'. The pads shine like burnished metal in the sunshine. Medium-sized water lily for pools and water gardens.

Nymphaea 'Marliacea Rubra Punctata' (1889, Latour-Marliac). Red magenta flowers mixed with carmine around red orange stamens. It is easy to grow and very floriferous. Edmund Sturtevant had founded his nursery in 1876, he became a regular correspondent. Latour-Marliac offered him a 20 per cent discount. Sturtevant was a 'Hollywood Pioneer' before the age of the silver screen, he set up the Cahuenga Water Gardens in the Los Angeles suburb of Hollywood primarily for tropical water lilies, stars and chorus line nymphs in their own way. Large water lily, suitable for ponds and lakes.

Nymphaea '**Conqueror**' (1910, Latour-Marliac) One of three reds introduced the year before Bory Latour-Marliac died. An apt epitaph for the man, many of whose hybridising conquests still survive and thrive. A large water lily with leaves of 16-20cm (6¼-7⅞in) and lively red 14cm (5½in) flowers nuanced with white. Suitable for large pools and ponds.

Nymphaea '**Phoebus**' (1909, Latour-Marliac). The attractive chestnut mottling on the leaves animate the final red copper sunset hue of the peony-shaped flowers. A small water lily, suitable for ponds and small lakes. Now very rare.

***Nymphaea* 'James Brydon** (1899, Dreer). One of the water lilies in Monet's second order dedicated to *Nymphaea*. The fuchsia red of the goblet shaped flowers can be glimpsed floating across his canvases. The emergent leaves are a dark purple. Medium-sized water lily that thrives in smaller sized ponds and pools. Nurseryman Henry Dreer and Latour-Marliac enjoyed a lengthy correspondence which continued with Édgard.

Nymphaea 'Atropurpurea' (1900, Latour-Marliac). Described by Latour-Marliac as 'the colour of veinous blood, very dark and whose shining petals are pointed into a hood at their extremity'. Sheldon strongly suspects that time has mixed the nomenclature so that it could be that the current 'Atropurpurea' is 'Gloriosa' and that 'Bateau' on the opening page is in fact 'Laydekeri Fulgens'. Medium-sized water lily, suitable for pools and ponds.

Nymphaea 'Marliacea Ignea' (1893, Latour-Marliac). It was introduced along with 'Marliacea Flammea', amply demonstrating Latour-Marliac's ability to succeed in breeding strong painter's palette shades of pink to red. Along with *N.* 'Robinsonii' Latour-Marliac wrote: '... remarkably hardy novelties which for six months of the year embellish the waters of pleasure grounds with their splendid flowers.' Medium-sized water lily that can also be grown in half barrels or smaller pools.

Nymphaea rubra. Latour-Marliac obtained this and the *N. odorata* and *tuberosa* in 1889 from the
American nurserman Edmund Sturtevant in the States. All three were used in his hybridising programmes.
One can understand Latour-Marliac's fascination with the dark reds of these medium-sized tropical water
lilies which look like crushed velvet set against the midnight blue pool at night.

Nymphaea 'Chateau Le Rouge'
(1972, Latour-Marliac). Some of
Latour-Marliac's original hybrids
appear to have been reinvented
under new names, it would seem to
be the case with current *N.*
'Chateau Le Rouge', which was
probably the original 'Atropurpurea'
in its first incarnation. Chateau le
Rouge was the birthplace of Bory
Latour-Marliac. The soundscape of
the nursery is dominated by several
species of croaking frogs. Medium-
sized water lily, suitable for small
ponds in partial shade.

Nymphaea 'Andréana' (1895, Latour-Marliac). The deep flushed petals forming a perfect frame for the lively egg yolk stamens. Rare, the modern Latour-Marliac nurseries are one of the few stockists. One plant will cover a square metre within the year. Small water lily, suitable for pools and tubs.

Above: *Nymphaea* 'Robinsonii' (1895, Latour-Marliac). After careful selection, Latour-Marliac celebrated his greatest ambassador in the English-speaking world – William Robinson. In 1901 Edmund Sturtevant wrote: 'A French hybrid which is indispensible in every good collection producing large flowers of the most brilliant dark orange-red.' Small water lily, suitable for ponds and lakes.

Right: *Nymphaea* 'Black Princess' (1998, Slocum). This large water lily is said to be a cross between a red hardy and a blue tropical. The pads can grow from 16 to 20cm (6¼-7⅞in) in diameter and the flowers 14cm (5½in). Described by Sheldon as: 'A truly exceptional lily.... For an original and eye-catching colour play, plant perennials like black-red hollyhocks, day lilies and bearded iris along the shore ...' Large water lily, suitable for lakes.

Below: *Nymphaea* 'Froebeli' (1898, Froebel). A blood-red water lily with olive green, distinctively spade-shaped leaves. Otto Froebel with whom Latour-Marliac was in correspondence, sent him one of the first plants. Easy to grow and suitable for small ponds and container gardens.

Facing page, top: *Nymphaea* 'Escarboucle' (1909, Latour-Marliac). A very large water lily similar in size to 'Black Princess'. A favourite of Latour-Marliac's which he recommended to all his best customers. Suitable for larger pools, ponds and lakes.

Facing page, bottom: *Nymphaea* 'La Vésuve' (1906, Latour-Marliac). Literally a brilliant large carmine red water lily matched in its volcanic associations with its contemporary 'Solfatare'. Relatively rare it is more exotic than 'Escarboucle'. Large water lily, suitable for bigger pools and ponds.

Pink

How to define pink? The delicacy of the colour associates with 'Maiden's Blush' and the tones of rosy, radiant, clear skin. Latour-Marliac's first pink hybrid in 1878 encapsulates blushes and scent, 'Odorata Exquisita' has 6cm (2⅜in) flowers that bloom profusely. In June 1887, when sending four plants of *Nymphaea odorata rosea* to George Nicholson of Kew, he described them as being baby pink and 'de toute beauté'. That sense of being in the first flush of youth is encapsulated in the name 'Candidissima Rosea', introduced by the American nurseryman, Edmund D. Sturtevant in 1884. There were several contemporary new pink-hued varieties he had not raised such as Henry T. Bahnson's large flowered pale pink fading to white 'Caroliniana', which was listed as his own hybrid in 1900 but has become devalued by self-seeding. Latour-Marliac had earlier improved it with the stronger pink 'Caroliniana Perfecta' in 1893 and then in 1908 the paler 'Caroliniana Rosea'.

His earliest pink, the large flowered 'Marliacea Carnea', was introduced in 1879, its blush petals surround yellow stamens. It was followed by the robust pure pink 'Marliacea Rosea' in 1887.

In 1893 he introduced 'Laydekeri Lilacea', which is still very beautiful for miniature gardens in tubs or barrels, little rosy lilac flowers deepening to a carmine pink. 1894 saw the arrival of 'Lucida' with large brilliant dark pink flowers whose colour deepens at the centre. Latour-Marliac's dedicated follower, Mrs Richmond enthused:

> 'Amongst the most beautiful of the newer water-lilies we may select … *Nymphaea Lucida* in delicate shades of salmon-pink, deeper in the centre, the blossoms being held erect about 6 inches above the water; it is a vigorous plant, with foliage marbled in brown, flowering during the whole season'.

Although available today it remains uncommon.

Lagrange introduced 'Laydekeri Rosea Prolifera' in 1895, which was only stocked until the 1920s but was reintroduced by the Davies in the 1990s. It is ideal for modern gardens as it has a mass of small rose magenta flowers on a white background, set against green sepals and leaves that thrive in small water pools less than 40cm (15¾in) deep. In 1899 Latour-Marliac introduced the pale pink 'Suavissima', whilst W.B. Shaw launched 'Odorata Luciana' one of the pink flowering forms described by Gertrude Jekyll in *Wall and Water Gardens* (1901).

In 1901 Latour-Marliac sent Robinson at Gravetye Manor 'a new *Nymphaea*, the 'Speciosa', which is the prettiest of all the pink *Nymphaea* in the freshness of its colour. The flowers are floating and scented with the appearance of the *Suavissima*, except that the latter has raised flowers and their colour is not as delicate'. It has survived at the nursery today but has become very rare.

As Jekyll wrote 'reputedly the giant of the races', the 1901 'Colossea' is a vigorous variety for large lakes that will root down to 1.5m (approx 5ft), it has large white flowers flushed with pale pink with pointed petals. 'Formosa', one of the most beautiful and rare Latour-Marliac hybrids, was introduced in 1907; followed in 1908 by 'Masaniello', with round, flushed pink and carmine flowers. The novelties for 1909 in shades of pink were the pretty little 'Galatée', coloured like an old rose flushed with white and with elegant foliage, and 'Somptuosa' with double crimson pink flowers fading on the outer petals. Two English scientists were celebrated in pale pink with 'Darwin' in 1909 and a year later 'Newton' in star-shaped flowers with long petals the reddish pink tips of which fade to white around sprawling stamens; in contrast, the 'Murillo' takes a dark pink form.

'James Hudson' was introduced in 1912, as were the following four pink water lilies: 'Goliath' with big pink flowers fading to white; the dark pink 'Nobilissima'; the white marked rose pink 'Eucharis'; and 'Lusitania', which has very floriferous old rose flowers fading to white. In 1913, the Latour-Marliac nursery continued to offer varieties such as the very floriferous 'Fabiola' with its hue of antique rose suffused with white, the ruffled double pink maturing to white flowers of 'Gloire du Temple-sur-Lot' and 'Marguerite Laplace' with large pink flowers that fade to white.

In 1914 a planet was chosen to give its name to the star-shaped 'Neptune' and the following year 'Tulipiformis', sporting enormous antique rose coloured flowers, made its debut. 'Tulipiformis' retains a stellar status as a most rare and sought after variety, attracting fees of €400 per plant when available. Introduced in 1924, 'Madame Wilfron Gonnère' has plump round double flowers flushed with pink on a white background with a deep pink heart. It is considered to be the most perfect of double pink *Nymphaea*. The Laydekers, who ran the Établissements Latour-Marliac, introduced a further four pinks in the 1930s; the rose-pink 'Baroness Orczy', 'Madame de Bonseigneur' with pale pink streaked flowers, the pale pink 'Madame Bory Latour-Marliac' and 'Princesse Elisabeth'.

In 1990 a new pink was introduced that is known both as 'Guy Maurel' and 'Jean Laydeker'. Perry Slocum introduced 'Ray Davies' in 1985, little did he realise that Davies would be a co-owner of the Établissements Latour-Marliac six years later. There are more water lilies described as pink than any others bred by Slocum, Perry, Marshall and Strawn a small further selection includes: 'Anna Epple' (1970, Epple), 'Berthold' (1992, Berthold), 'Celebration' (1994, Strawn) 'Millennium Pink' (2000, Dorset), 'Norma Gedye' (1972, Gedye), and 'Pink Glory' (c.1960, Beldt).

Facing page: *Nymphaea* 'Murillo' (1910, Latour-Marliac). A medium-sized water lily whose flowers are a similar shape to 'Ellisiana'. Easy to grow but rarely found outside Latour-Marliac.

Above: *Nymphaea* 'Formosa' (1900, Latour-Marliac). First exhibited at the 1900 *Exposition Universelle*, Latour-Marliac had intended to dedicate it to Architecte Girault. Rare and beautiful it re-appeared as 'Formosa' in 1907. Full soft lilac pink flowers darkening towards the centre with white sepals and yellow stamens. Medium-sized water lily, suitable for pools and ponds.

Facing page, top: *Nymphaea* 'Princess Elizabeth' (1939, Latour-Marliac). Launched as 'Princesse Elisabeth' the then Princess Elizabeth admired the first plants growing in the water lily pool at Windsor Castle. The 10cm (4in) flowers are cyclamen pink, orange stamens and a delicate perfume. Easy maintenance, develops gently and is free flowering. Medium-sized water lily, suitable for pools and ponds.

Facing page, bottom: *Nymphaea* 'Pink Sunrise' (1993, Strawn). This large water lily has 12cm (4¾in) double bright pink flowers set against pads of 14-20cm (5½-7¾in). Eye-catching and dramatic, it was one that made Strawn's reputation in the water lily world. Suitable for pools and water gardens.

Above: *Nymphaea* 'Spectabilis' (1900, Latour-Marliac). Launched at the 1900 *Exposition Universelle*. A rare variety whose 10cm (4in) flowers have different tones of pink and white. Medium-sized water lily, suitable for pools and ponds. In 1905 Latour-Marliac wrote to William Robinson that he did not think it would be a commercial success as it did not shoot well. It is still available!

Facing page, top: *Nymphaea* 'Gloire du Temple-sur-Lot' (1913, Latour-Marliac). The shape differed from all other Latour-Marliac raisings. The pale pink scented flowers fade to white, they are large with a multitude of lively petals. Édgard guaranteed that it would create a sensation. Large water lily, suitable for pools, ponds and lakes.

Facing page, bottom: *Nymphaea* 'Newton' (1910, Latour-Marliac). The very large star-shaped 14cm (5½in) blooms nestle attractively against its 16-20cm (6¼-7⅞in) green pads. The flowers were described as pink-vermilion, the petals long and straight with white sepals and reddish orange stamens. Large water lily that thrives in deep water. Suitable for larger pools, ponds and lakes.

Overleaf: *Nymphaea* 'Amabilis' (1921, Latour-Marliac). Like many of Latour-Marliac's final hybrids, 'Amabilis' did not set viable seed, it is generally accepted that he worked towards this outcome in order to stop further experimentation with his hybrids. One of 3 novelties introduced by Édgard in 1921 the salmon-pnk star-shaped 'Amabilis' literally means 'lovely'. Large, vigorous water lily that thrives in deep water.

Nymphaea '*Guy Maurel*' (1990, Latour-Marliac). This large water lily was discovered by employee Guy Maurel on the Latour-Marliac site, probably an overlooked seedling from the same cross that bore the rare 'Tulipiformis'. Large water lily with flowers from 16-20cm (6¼-7⅞in) it is suitable for larger pools and ponds.

Nymphaea 'Laydekeri Rosea Prolifera' (1895, Lagrange). Stocked at the Latour-Marliac nurseries until 1920 and then re-introduced by the Davies because it is ideal for pools in smaller modern gardens. It has a multitude of small rosy magenta flowers. As its name suggests, it was bred from one of Latour-Marliac's hybrids 'L. Rosea'.

Nymphaea 'Amabilis' (1921, Latour-Marliac). There is a delightful symmetry in this star-shaped water lily. Classed as salmon-pink, mauve hues appear as it matures. See the previous double page spread to appreciate the way it colonises the water surface. Floriferous. Thrives in deep water.

Nymphaea 'Eugène de Land' (1913, Shaw). Listed originally as 'Eugènia de Lande' when an engraving was sent from America by William Tricker to Latour-Marliac. This more romantic name was retained by fellow American nurseryman W. B. Shaw in 1925. However, the name has now been anglicised. Medium-sized water lily, suitable for pools and ponds.

Nymphaea 'Sylphida' (1912, Latour-Marliac) Selected by Édgard in 1913 as one of the water lilies sent to M Laplace to represent the Établissement Latour-Marliac in the Bagatelle gardens, as well as by Barr & Sons for an exhibition at Holland House. As opposed to a nymph, a winged sylph or *sylphide* in French evokes for many the romantic tragic ballet. This 'Sylphida' has deep pink flowers streaked with white. It is now extremely rare and difficult to find.

Nymphaea 'Goliath' (1912, Latour-Marliac). Édgard Latour-Marliac fought a lengthy court case to establish Goliath as his father's work. As the name suggests they are large with flowers of 15cm (6in) and 15-20cm (6-7⅞in) pads. Suitable for lakes.

Overleaf: *Nymphaea* 'Fabiola' (1908, Latour-Marliac). Still advertised as a novelty as late as 1913. Amos Perry stocked 'Fabiola' in England stating: 'large open fls. Brilliant pink, flaked and striped white and rose, with bright mahogany stamens, fls. Produced in great profusion throughout the season. Ex. fine'. Large water lily, suitable for pools and ponds.

Above: *Nymphaea* 'Rose Arey' (1913, Fowler). Introduced by L. Helen Shaw Fowler, the daughter of Walter Shaw. She had taken over his nursery, W.B. Shaw near Washington DC, in 1913. It was awarded a silver medal by the New York Horticultural Society. The deep pink lilac flowers are fragrant. Large water lily, suitable for growing in a large container or small lily pool.

Facing page top: *Nymphaea* 'Neptune' (1914, Latour-Marliac). Also known as 'Larroque'. Exotic star shaped crimson pink flowers that fade to old rose and white, and with sepals that are white and pink whilst the purple foliage ages to olive green. Medium-sized water lily, suitable for containers and small pools.

Facing page bottom: *Nymphaea* 'Madame Maurice Laydeker' (1936, Latour-Marliac). Named for Bory and Alida's daughter Angèle, wife of Maurice Laydeker. Still classed as a novelty in 1939, her son Jean Laydeker described the flowers as *forme globuleuse* (globular form). A medium-sized water lily with 12-16cm (4¾-6¼in) leaves and 10cm (4in) flowers. Suitable for pools and ponds.

Nymphaea 'Tulipiformis' (1921, Latour-Marliac). Édgard originally selected this water lily to name for René Gérard but it was slow to multiply. Like the famed 17th century Tulipomania when the value of rare tulip bulbs reached the stratosphere, in water lily terms 'Tulipiformis' could be classed as a modern rival. Such is their rarity that they often attain prices of €400 each. Large water lily suitable for bigger pools and water gardens.

Above: *Nymphaea* 'Odorata Exquisita' (1878, Latour-Marliac). This small water lily was exhibited at both the 1889 and 1900 *Expositions Universelles* in Paris. A small pink with an excellent Latour-Marliac pedigree for small pools and containers.

Facing page, top: *Nymphaea* 'Millennium Pink' (2000, Dorset Water Lily Company). It is similar to 'Amabilis', with star-shaped flowers that are exceptionally pointed. Large water lily, suitable for pools and ponds.

Facing page, bottom: *Nymphaea* 'Celebration' (1994, Strawn). A medium sized water lily with glorious fuchsia coloured blooms for smaller ponds and pools. There is something to celebrate in the beauty of this lovely water lily as it rises up from the depths. The deep fuchsia-pink petals are almost transparent in the sunlight. The talented Dr Kirk Strawn introduced this water lily, three years after he retired as a lecturer at the Texas A&M University. Both Ray Davies and Robert Sheldon cite him as the only person to come close to the hybridising skills of Latour-Marliac.

Nymphaea 'Laydekeri Fulgens' (1893, Latour-Marliac). The colour was described by Latour-Marliac as amaranth today warm shades of pink deepening to carmine. Early flowering, easy to grow and blooms May to October. Medium-sized water lily, suitable for pools and ponds.

Nymphaea 'Mme Wilfron Gonnére' (1924, Latour-Marliac). Introduced by Édgard and named for his maternal grandmother, Euphrasine de la Marsalle Gonnére. The 10cm (4in) clear pink flowers nestle amongst green pads of 12-15cm (4½-6in). A voluptuous medium-sized easy-to-grow water lily for pools and small ponds.

Nymphaea 'Speciosa'
(1899, Latour-Marliac). A
medium-sized water lily whose
reddish white petals are broad
and pointed. Rarely found
outside Latour-Marliac. Suitable
for small pools.

The Elusive Blue

Latour-Marliac hybridised tropical colours into a kaleidoscope of hardy hues but the colour blue remained elusively tropical. In 1889 he had requested seed of *Nymphaea zanzibariensis* from Kew and exchanges continued until 1897. Monet and Gertrude Jekyll shared a curious combination of coincidences – they both trained as artists, acquired their final gardens in 1883, suffered from poor eyesight and gardened with painterly gusto. They are amongst many who corresponded with Latour-Marliac in the hope of successfully planting their pools in hardy blue sensations.

Monet went one step further by trying to create frost free, heated conditions within his water garden at Giverny with the sheltered back-up of his extensive greenhouse. One each of *N. zanzibariensis* and *N. stellata* were despatched on 27th May 1898. Although Monet had started painting the surface composition of his pond, blues are nowhere to be seen.

On 6th September 1900 Jekyll made her first contact as co-editor of *The Garden* – they were interested in featuring and illustrating Latour-Marliac's new varieties. After responding with delight, he addressed the vexed question of growing hardy blue water lilies: 'Following the beautiful flower with deep blue flowers of which you write and which has flowered well in the open air in England. Here is what I can tell you about it: … it is the issue of a new breed that I have obtained from seeds often taken from *Nymphaea zanzibariensis* and which have given me a crowd of varieties, many more resistant than the type, coloured with rich nuances of dark blue, pale blue, deep violet, clear violet, bright pink, light pink, lilac, etc.

Unfortunately these plants do not send up shoots from the base and their numerous varieties do not come true to type from seed; it is therefore impossible to fix them and name them. As to their hardiness, it is not guaranteed, that is to say that they perish during the winter; but it is already a considerable achievement that they grow and flourish very well during the summer outdoors in an English climate, just as do the *Nymphaea stellata* and *scutifolia*, which are well behind in equalling them in beauty. Seeing that these new varieties of *N. zanzibariensis* interest you I will send you by post a few sprays of flowers and leaves; some of these flowers have blue sepals. The leaves are dentate and mostly very big and also variegated which suit the colouring of the flowers. I am sorry to have only sent you flowers from young plants, but the strongest have been sent to Paris.'

This was to the 1900 *Exposition Universelle*. Initially, much to Latour-Marliac's disappointment, the architect Girault had implied that the addition of blue water lilies would be too much. On 16th June, politely indignant, Latour-Marliac noted the change of heart and added that the six selected were varieties he had bred from *N. zanzibariensis*. They would require fresh water, warmed by the sun, and once settled would flower into October. Although not a propitious site, he was allocated 75 square metres by the Grand Palais and various small *bassins* at the Peti Palais. He was persuasive and the blues joined the throng, a sight echoed during 2013. In 1907 Latour–Marliac introduced the tender *N. zanzibariensis* 'Azurea'.

In an undated 1970s edition of *Sud-Ouest*, L.-G. Gayan reported: 'M Jean Laydeker maintains the secrets of his grandfather and pursues success. … A world secret. Out of 60 annual trials, the percentage of varieties retained will be about 10 per cent – the chosen few remain a mystery for the next 6 years. Blue is still the prize. He has not given his name to any varieties'.

In 2007, as Robert Sheldon took over the nurseries, and one hundred and twenty years after Latour-Marliac eulogised about crossing cultural boundaries in every sense to enamel water surfaces with his hardy nymphs in *Des Nymphaeas et Nelumbiums Rustiques*, across the world in Thailand Pairat Songpanich, a disciple and admirer of Bory Latour-Marliac, introduced *N.* 'Siam Blue Hardy'. Songpanich had started his hybridisation journey in 2003, it would have to be an intersubgeneric cross, a process as complex as it sounds. Finally the resolutely tropical blue, despite differing chromosome numbers from the robust genus, was to be matched, hatched and despatched. Taking a hardy *Nymphaea* as the pod parent, Songpanich crossed with pollen from the tropical blue-flowering sub-genus *Brachyceras*, this coupling yielded pods with a few fertile seeds that were germinated. As the seedlings matured, one amongst them manifested the smooth leaves of its hardy parent whilst the long flowering stems of its *Brachyceras* genes supported a purplish blue bloom. It was genetically confirmed by Dr Vipa Hongtrakul after which it was launched onto the waiting water lily world. How apt that the Latour-Marliac site was the first water lily nursery in Europe to offer the new blue hues of its progeny to the general public. Blues that warm towards the regal with shades of purple and royal blue. The corks must have been popping in celestial paradise.

Facing page, top: *Nymphaea* 'Siam Purple 2' (2011, Songpanich). This lily was the winner of the International Water Garden Society 'New Water Lily Competition' in 2011. In the run up to the competition 'Siam Purple 2' was grown alongside other novelties in The Sarah P. Duke Gardens in Durham, North Carolina. Judging took place in September. Medium-sized water lily, suitable for pools and smaller water gardens.

Facing page, below: *Nymphaea* 'Queen Sirikit' (2007, Songpanich). Latour-Marliac was content to class purple as a shade of blue, an unchanging interpretation in the world of water lilies. The flowers are up to 15cm (6in) across. Queen Sirikit is consort of the King of Thailand Bhumibol Adulyadej, and her background is one of cultural exchange with her father having served in Thai embassies in Washington DC, London and Paris. She is an active patron of Thailand's conservation work, especially with native plant species. Medium-sized water lily, suitable for pools and smaller water gardens.

Monet's Water Lilies

'Damascened with large round leaves of water lilies, encrusted with the precious stones that are their flowers, this water seems, when the sun plays upon its surface, the masterpiece of a goldsmith who has combined the alloys of the most magical metals.' Arsene Alexandre', *Le Figaro* 1901

The quoted setting is that of Monet's new water garden at Giverny, decanted from the vintage blending of the water lily genus by the ingenuity of Bory. While many more water lilies would be introduced by Latour-Marliac's son, son-in-law and grandson, it is the name Monet which has come forever to reflect water lilies – their depiction on canvas flowing onto postcards and souvenirs that have been lapped up by galleries, homes and gardens across the globe.

Monet was by no means Latour-Marliac's best contemporary customer, but he has become the most significant name in the Le Temple-sur-Lot archives. His name appears just eight times between 1894 and 1908. Monet's first order illustrates that he has a new pond requiring diversified planting, with water lilies only appearing on the second page.

In May 1883 Monet had moved with Alice Hoschedé, his two sons and her six children to the Maison du Pressoir in the centre of the village of Giverny in Normandy.

Below: Giverny – Monet had moved there in 1883, and by 1889 his studio was still in the house and he was yet to acquire the water meadows beyond.

Facing page: Monet in clear focus in contrast with the dreamy quality of the water lilies artistically distributed on the mirror of his pond.

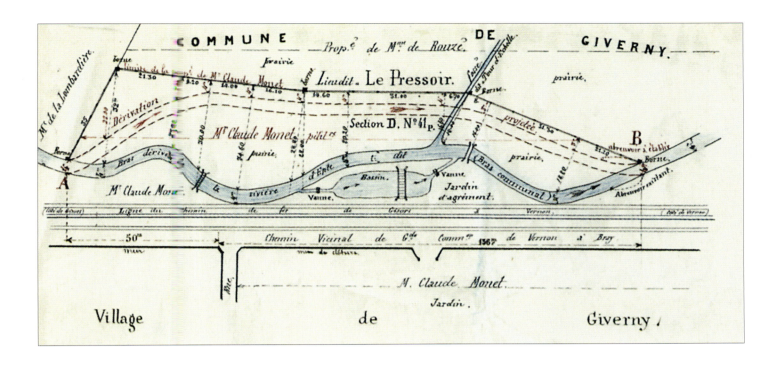

The gardens were walled and Monet rapidly set about organising the enclosure into a series of rectangular beds for his impressive massed plantings whose flowers caught the east to west arc of the sun throughout the day. He softened the central walk by pruning away the branches off the trunks of the established spruces that lined it, training climbing roses up and around them. The bases of their trunks were disguised with raised 'carp-back' beds filled with drifting flowers and, during August and September, the final horticultural illusion was achieved when the path was lost under waves of nasturtiums. Instead of a typically French formal allée, Monet managed to create a living verdant tunnel.

Monet was a regular reader of the journal *Le Jardin*, a comprehensive twice yearly tome founded by Godefroy-Lebeuf (to whom he had been introduced by Gustave Caillebotte) in 1887 on all matters horticultural. Lengthy in-depth papers ranged from French beans to orchids, from Paris to the world, from pests and diseases to glasshouses, interspersed with news and a who's who of gardeners, botanists and designers. In 1887 *Le Jardin* included a lengthy paper by Latour-Marliac entitled *Notice sur les Nymphæs et Nelumbiums*. The opening lines of the *Notice* are like a prelude to Monet's *magnum opus*:

An important revolution has been undertaken in the bathing beauty plant world: the beautiful nymphs of warmer climes have eased their rigorous and cold disdainful aloofness …for fecund alliances with our own hardy water lilies, and have now given birth to multi-coloured hybrids with an absolute robustness that will withstand northerly winds and sub-zero temperatures. …

The *Nelumbium* … with their great upstanding leaves create a verdant bosquet, decorated with enormous flowers and delectable fragrance. The softly scented *Aponogeton*, the *Villarsia*, the *Lymnocharis*, the *Nuphar*, the *Trapa natans* and *verbanensis* (the latter with deep red petioles and veins), all have a favoured place in this special reserve.'

In 1893 Monet bought a piece of meadowland directly below his house and garden in Giverny. It was traversed by the tiny River Ru (a small tributary of the River Epte) which he intended to divert in order to create a pond.

As artist and gardener, Monet understood the value of framing his water picture: contrasting soft green banks with the architectural accents of marginal aquatics sinuously

Facing page: Monet diverted the tiny River Ru to feed his first pond. Little did the authorities know that the original pond would almost treble in size.

Above: Monet's plan for diverting the River Ru to create a pond in his garden at Giverny. The pond today is far larger than shown on the plan and to the left of the bridge.

Left: The first page of Monet's 1894 order for a colourful array of aquatic plants. Water lilies and lotuses featured on the second page.

Facing page, top: *Nymphaea* 'Atropurpurea'. Monet might well have seen this when he attended the 1900 *Exposition Universelle* in Paris where it was launched. Its colour is described as rouge noirâtre or dark blackish red. Apart from *N.* 'Robinsonii', the archives show that Latour-Marliac had intended to rename *N.* 'Atropurpurea' for 'a friend' or Charles Girault. However, in a letter to Girault enclosing the list of plants for the 1900 *Exposition Universelle*, he sought Girault's permission to call a *Nymphaea* 'Architecte Girault' or 'Radiosa' if he declined. 'Atropurpurea' is the only variety to have survived.

Facing page, bottom: Monet ordered five lotus varieties. Latour-Marliac captured the beauty of the *Nelumbium* when he wrote: '... they can equally contribute to the embellishment of sheets of water ... with their great upstanding leaves create a verdant bosquet, decorated with enormous flowers and delectable fragrance'.

enclosing the colourful water lilies and reflective surface. He followed the naturalistic principle of planting in odd numbers and ordered three each of 23 different aquatic plants from Latour-Marliac.

In the upper garden at Giverny, Monet designed to deceive the eye and manipulate the horizon. Reading his first order you appreciate that he intended to exercise this principle for the margins of his pool. The creeping perennial pennywort, *Hydrocotyle vulgaris*, with its neat rounded foliage tinted with pink flowers, carpets boggy ground vigorously as does its more elegant and floriferous cousin from the sea shores of Argentina, *Hydrocotyle bonariensis*. Monet ordered the invasive white variegated ribbon grass *Arundinaria picta*, (now *Phalaris arundinacea* 'Picta') whose French common name is Shepherd's ribbon. For additional grass-like effect there was the northern long sedge, *Carex folliculata*, and the cotton grasses, broad-leaved *Eriophorum latifolia*, and tussock forming *E. Scheuchzeri*. Bullrushes would fringe the pond naturalistically and stabilise the banks, he selected the sea club rush, *Scirpus maritimus*, now *Bulboschoenus maritimus*,

and *Scirpus radicans*, now *Schoenoplectus radicans*.

William Robinson, in later editions of *The English Garden*, enthused about the arrowheads, *Sagittaria*, named for their elegant lance-shaped leaves, as 'graceful water-plants not only charming at the waterside, but from their structure among the most interesting of hardy perennials'. Monet chose the white flowering *S. gracilis* (now *S. latifolia*) and the reed mace, *Typha stenophylla*, (now *T. laxmannii*) which Robinson described as 'Graceful water-plants, hardy, easily grown, and very ornamental ... *T. stenophylla* with narrow leaves turned in a spiral and short thick spikes.' In addition he ordered another Robinson recommendation, *Pontederia montevidensis* (now *Sagittaria montevidensis*).

The bright yellow flowers of *Caltha polypetala* (now *Caltha palustris* var *palustris*) would have heralded spring, followed by the yellow loosestrife, *Lysimachia vulgaris* and *Sisyrinchium sulfureum* (now *S. californicum*). As the name suggests the golden club, *Orontium aquaticum*, has a multiplicity of bright yellow tipped spadices that look like candles which fade with age to white, set on a rosette of sage green leaves. Lizard's Tail, the common name for

Above: *Nymphaea* 'William Falconer' has leaves that look like burnished metal (with red veining that does not show in this image) out of which emerge deep garnet ruby coloured flowers with sparkling stamens and an egg yolk yellow centre. Writing to Robinson, Latour-Marliac described 'William Falconer' which was introduced by Henry Dreer as '… very distinguished but its deep colour is lost in bright sunshine and burns'. The dappled shade of Monet's willows suited it.

Right: *Nymphaea* 'Arethusa' like 'William Falconer', was also bred by Henry Dreer around 1899 and he introduced it in 1902. Its large full flowers are described as being bright crimson and they look lighter in the sunshine. Monet was not the only keen customer, during 1905 Latour-Marliac ran out of stock.

Nymphaea 'James Brydon'. With its excessively double crimson-pink flowers enabling it to catch shafts of light from all angles you can understand why this *Nymphaea* attracted Monet's attention. It had been introduced by Dreer in 1901, at the time they were employing William Tricker until he re-established his own business in Arlington, New Jersey in 1906.

members of the Saururaceae, aptly describes the dense, rather scaly tail-like, ivory-white inflorescences with the bonus of being fragrant that share the luminous quality of the sea holly, *Eryngium*. Monet selected three species: the *Gymnotheca chinensis*, which is native to south-east China; the swamp lily *Saururus cernuus*, and *S. loureiri*, (now *S. chinensis* (Loureiro)). In contrast, with clumped stems rising to 3.6m, is the Manchurian Wild Rice, *Hydropyrum latifolium* (now *Zizania latifolia*), also from China.

Monet ordered five varieties of lotus: *Nelumbium album*, *N. japonicum roseum*, *N. luteum*, *N.* 'Osiris', *N. speciosum roseum* and three water lilies: the yellow flowering *Nymphaea* 'Flava', *N.* 'Odorata Sulphurea Grandiflora' and *N.* 'Laydekeri Rosea', the latter in *The English Garden* Robinson described as:

'One of the most useful of hardy Water-Lilies, with fragrant, pale pink flowers, passing through several shades to deep rose as they fade away. It does best in shallow water and gives so few offsets that several plants should be grouped to secure the full effect of the changing flowers.'

On the water, the pink flowers of the *Nymphaea* 'Laydekeri Rosea', *Nelumbium japonicum roseum* and *N. speciosum roseum* would have mingled with those of the willow grass or water knotweed, *Polygonum amphibium*. Apart from the textural greens of the water lily leaves, verdant contrasts would be provided by the glossy dark green floating rosettes of water chestnuts, *Trapa natans* and *T. verbonensis* (originating from Lake Maggiore and now classed with *T. natans*). There would also have been the bright yellow-green or blue-green floating leaves of the frost-tender parrot feather, *Myriophyllum proserpinacoides*, (now *M. aquaticum*). How well it would have survived the winter is unknown.

Monet had a large greenhouse where tender plants could be overwintered so this might have been an annual task.

Monet's hopes might have been raised when he read the *Le Jardin* report of the unseasonally warm weather towards the end of 1897 and early 1898. Despite this warmth Monet had to create frost free, heated conditions within his water garden at Giverny. Monet had one each of *Nymphaea zanzibariensis* and *N. stellata* delivered to Giverny, but they failed.

Monet travelled up and down to the 1900 *Exposition Universelle* in Paris from Giverny. When it closed on 12th November, Monet followed up a suggestion from the dealer Durand-Ruel to create 'an important show' dedicated entirely to his work from 1889 to 1900. After frustrating months in early 1900 painting his 'Londons', he returned to Giverny and with comparative ease finished six out of twelve Water Lily pond canvases that he had begun in the summer of 1899. From April to November he completed a further nine views: unlike the unpredictable smog in London, water lilies could be relied on to flower for months. A fact much vaunted by Latour-Marliac and proved during the *Exposition*.

Monet's exhibition opened on 22nd November, 1900, the first to take Latour-Marliac's hybrids from colour plates to high art. Monet's output without and within his garden was traced in 26 paintings. The viewer started without, but thirteen paintings entered the gardens where the water lily pond could be seen publicly for the first time. The critic Julien Leclerq viewed this exhibition as a continuation of the enlightened thinking of 18th-century France, where painters and philosophers were united in their veneration of nature. Here was a personal consultation with the genius of the place that enabled a revealing of their deepest sensibilities. The usually favourable critic, Arsène Alexandre, was damning on the inclusion of a lily pond until he visited Monet's gardens in 1901 and wrote an enraptured article for *Le Figaro*.

The Japanese Footbridge was first publically exhibited in November 1900, what we see is the product of new garden pride – the weeping willows, the arching bridge, the glassy mirror of the water reflecting the canopy but bejeweled by Latour-Marliac's water nymphs, fleshy pink, cream and yellow. Like Monet the water lily responds to light. The lily pads burnished in the sun and the pond framed by the marginal plants Latour-Marliac also supplied. As Gustave Geffroy wrote: 'It is in Giverny that he has created his special garden by diverting the course of a small tributary of the River Epte. He has created a tiny pond with ever clear waters surrounded with his choice of trees, shrubs, and flowers, and decorated its

surface with diverse coloured water lilies which emerge in spring amongst large leaves, and which bloom throughout the summer. Above this flourishing water, is a light wooden Japanese styled bridge, and the air itself plays through the trees, the slightest breeze, the nuances of every hour, all images that calm the surrounding natural environment. …

With his water landscapes, where the seasonal flowers appear in the soft and precious enchantment of light manipulated by space, Claude Monet presents us with a magic mirror which we have never seen before, where his artist's genius is resplendent and beams with the beauty of the earth and sky.'

Opposite page: Today's visitor to Giverny approaches the pond from behind the Japanese Bridge. The bridge had neither upper canopy nor wisteria. The bamboo to the right became a retreat from which Monet could watch the water and what he called his water nymphs – the water lilies.

Below: *The Japanese Footbridge,* 1900, ablaze with colour and sunshine.

Left: *Pond with Water Lilies* or *The Water Lily Pond* 1904. By 1904 Monet had tripled the size of his pond and ordered new deeper-coloured expensive hybrids from Latour-Marliac. After ten years of observation his painting has matured from a garden record into an exploration of the ever changing harmony of colours played out amongst the shimmer and mirror of the water surface. The banks have almost disappeared, only the surface as growing medium and mirror remain.

Facing page: Monet at work on *Les Grande Décorations*, a section of which can be seen on pages 6-7.

By 1904 Monet was a wealthy man and had arguably created a unique setting. At Giverny the water garden had matured into a work of art, a fusion of the artist's consummate eye and plantsman's skills. For this canvas Monet ordered four new, expensive water lilies on 26th May. Only one was hybridised by Latour-Marliac, *Nymphaea* 'Atropurpurea', which had been exhibited at the 1900 *Exposition Universelle*.

The *N.* 'Arethusa' had been bred by Henry Dreer. Dreer had also bred *N.* 'William Falconer' and *N.* 'James Brydon'. On 27th April 1907 Monet wrote to his agent, Paul Durand-Ruel that, although he does not wish currently to exhibit his water lily canvases, painting them gives him great pleasure.

The start of 1910 was depressing for Monet who was in anguish over the poor state of his wife Alice's health and the terrible floods that had encroached halfway up his upper garden. In a letter on 10th February to Durand Ruel:

'... I thought for a while that my entire garden would be destroyed and I was very concerned. Finally the water receded little by little, and although I've lost a lot of plants, it will probably be less calamitous than I'd feared. But what a disaster all the same ...'

After Alice's death, the bamboo thicket beyond the Japanese Bridge overlooking his sinuous pool populated by water lilies became Monet's refuge and seat of inspiration. In the following fifteen years his own battle with cataracts, the death of his elder son and the toll of the Great War found expression through his painting. In all, Monet painted over 250 canvases of his water lilies.

While Latour-Marliac's remarkable water lily legacy is much less celebrated than Monet's, the innovative results from his pools at Le Temple-sur-Lot enabled Monet to cultivate his water garden, bring its flourishing success into his atelier at Giverny and from there to the world. Their legacies are inextricably intertwined. A key reason why Monet made water lilies the centrepiece of his life's work, as well as his bequest to the nation of France, was no doubt their aesthetic beauty and, more pragmatically, lengthy flowering season. In addition, as one of Latour-Marliac's customers, Monet's lily pond was quite literally one of the first in the world to be naturalised with colourful, as opposed to simple white, water lilies. His skills had been honed by the play of light on haystacks, poplars and other subjects without his garden, then irises and roses within, but now he had created a revolutionary scene that could not be painted by any other artist.

More than their beauty, this originality could explain why he protected it the way he did by allowing only close friends and family to behold it. In their turn the water lilies offered a dazzling solace.

Les Grandes Décorations

One hundred years ago Europe was riven by its Great War, the letters of Latour-Marliac's son and heir, Édgard, describe the desolation and devastation of their small rural community. Monet too old to fight, painted and gardened, he allowed himself to be filmed at work in his water garden.

On 15th January 1915 when the vast Third Atelier was built near the house in Giverny, Monet outlined its purpose to fellow Japanese print enthusiast and founder of the Societé des Amis du Louvre, Raymond Koechlin: '…I sometimes feel ashamed that I am devoting myself to artistic pursuits while so many of our people are suffering and dying for us. It's true that fretting never did any good. So I am pursuing my idea of the *Grande Décoration*. … it's the project that I've had in mind for some time now: water, water-lilies, plants, spread over a huge surface.'

In the final twelve years of his life he played out his emotions on canvas after canvas in the vast brutalist third atelier at Giverny, not least on over 40 great canvas panels, 22 of which were placed on stretchers measuring 2 x 3m, 2 x 4.25m, or 2 x 6m. After his death in 1926, 90 metres of these painted sensations that he had selected were transferred to the Musee de l'Orangerie, Paris.

At his own request the *Grandes Décorations*, better known as *Les Nymphéas*, were not hung until after his death. Clemenceau had suggested hanging them in the Musée de l'Orangerie in Paris, and took an active role in ensuring that the architect Camille Lefévre created a suitable setting. Visitors descended from the vestibule into two subtly Art Deco oval galleries, they were decorated, almost seamlessly, with Monet's capture of green reflections, blue reflections, sun rise, sunset, furrowed willow trees, all in and around his tranquil water. Although the Musée underwent extensive renovation from 2000-2006, today's visitor can still walk right up to follow each brushstroke or sit in quiet contemplation (crowds permitting!) of the entire scene.

The power of experiencing *Les Grandes Décorations*, the water lily canvases that line the ovoid walls in the basement of the Musee de l'Orangerie, is the illusion of being immersed at all hours of the day with flowering nymphs scattered by Botticelli's Flora. Monet had watched their every sensation for thirty years, the last ten spellbound by the infinitesimal reflections played out on the watery canvas of flowers, buds and pads. As Geffroy wrote: 'In front of the luminous abyss of the pool of *Nymphéas*, he formulated, reprised, and once more reformulated this unending measurement of his life's dream and unceasing quest for his art. He found there, for want of a better phrase, the last word, if such things can have a first and last word. He discovered and demonstrated that *tout est partout* – all is everywhere, and that after having run round the world in adoration of the light which clarifies all, he came to know that this light was reflected in all its splendour and mysteries from the bamboos, irises and roses in the mirror of water across which pour the strange flowers that seem the most silent and most secretive of all other flowers.'

CHAPTER 4

Nurseryman to the World:
A Good Customer Base

As far as aquatic plants and especially Nymphaea are concerned, I am convinced that I will next operate a revolution in the ornamentation of lakes, pools and outdoor aquariums by obtaining several very hardy hybrids that will possess all the rich colours of the most remarkable subtropical Nymphaea.'

B. Latour-Marliac to William Robinson, 3rd August 1887

Beyond the Bamboo Curtain

Education and financial security enabled Latour-Marliac to socialise with ease amongst his customers – titled, scientific, commercial or amateur. Although the surviving correspondence is one sided, the early years record more than commerce; the confirmation and despatch of orders are often accompanied by comments and notes. There was a marked increase in business and new introductions or 'nouveautés' following the 1889 *Exposition Universelle* in Paris. This led to friendships amongst patrons, gardeners and journalists in France, England and America, several of whom made the journey to Le Temple-sur-Lot.

The English developed into his best customers, largely thanks to William Robinson's writings which were enjoyed in all English speaking countries across the British Empire and the United States. In his quest for as wide a range of *Nymphaea* as possible Latour-Marliac was in early correspondence and exchange with American growers such as William Tricker and Henry Dreer, and to a lesser extent Edward Sturtevant and the Olmsted Brothers. The great gardener and author Gertrude Jekyll, the Rothschild Head Gardener James Hudson and the Editor of *The Queen* Mrs Richmond are key English names. After Latour-Marliac's death in 1911, the latter two were still in regular touch with his son Édgard who introduced the *Nymphaea* 'James Hudson' in 1912. Many English nurseries ordered wholesale quantities and when working through the correspondence, it is astounding to see how many months

---

Previous page: Tropical water lilies colonise one of the original pans in summer providing a foreground, from left to right, for the building housing the prune drying oven, Édgard Latour-Marliac's villa and the modernised 'apartment'. Édgard writes about a 'chalet' on site, it is difficult to decide whether it is the building to the left or the right of his villa.

Facing page: A very oriental-style front cover for Latour-Marliac's 1906 catalogue. The Japanese display at the 1900 *Exposition Universelle* was a forerunner for the much larger 1910 Japanese-British exhibition. It heralds his prizes at the 1889 and 1900 Paris *Expositions* as well as the honour of receiving the British Veitch Memorial Medal.

elapsed between the despatch of orders and final settlement. Many of these customers who typically received plants in spring, are sent reminders to settle their outstanding accounts months later in November, December or even the following January.

After 1889, when Latour-Marliac had showed the nine new water lilies of 'his own raising' to so much acclaim at the *Exposition Universelle* in Paris, he introduced a stunning succession of ever better types. Between 1889 and his death in 1911, out of a total of seventy-one new varieties introduced, five water lilies were named to celebrate and thank his customers and associates.

Before the 1889 *Exposition Universelle* the Latour-Marliac archives are filled with scientific enquiry often laced with chatty correspondence. After the *Exposition* the tone was more businesslike and more focused. Some of his most loyal French clients included French critic, novelist and journalist, Jean-Baptiste Alphonse Karr alongside various grandees such as the Comte de Castillon, plus the Comte (Alfred-Louis-Marie) de Noailles, a regular customer firstly for bamboo in 1882, 1887 and 1888, and then for water lilies as well. Noailles introduced the Comte d'Epremesnil who placed several orders. And so this pattern continued. Many of Latour-Marliac's original bamboo customers had sizeable estates and they in turn planted up their lakes and fashioned pools for water lilies.

Over in England at Shrubland Park, about ninety miles north of London, James St Vincent, later Fourth Baron de Saumarez, had married Jane Ann Broke and they inherited the Shrubland estate from her uncle in 1837. Saumarez appears early in the archives and his career dovetails with the development of Latour-Marliac's nursery. It is no exaggeration to say that one letter in February 1887 in which Saumarez suggested contacting William Robinson lies at the root of Latour-Marliac's global success.

On 1st May 1891 a delighted Latour-Marliac sent Saumarez ('Milord') his catalogue of aquatic plants, on which he marked the hardiest water lilies with an X and confirmed that the Marliacea varieties were truly floriferous from July onwards. 3 *N.* 'Marliacea Albida , 1 *N.* 'Marliacea

1906

ÉTABLISSEMENT HORTICOLE

Du TEMPLE-SUR-LOT (Lot-et-Garonne)

✳ ✳ ✳

SPÉCIALITÉ DE NYMPHÆAS  ET AUTRES PLANTES AQUATIQUES

B. LATOUR-MARLIAC

Officier d'Académie

DIRECTEUR

Obtenteur d'un Premier Prix à l'Exposition Universelle de 1889
et d'une Médaille d'Or à celle de 1900
et gratifié aussi en 1898 de la Grande Médaille du Weitch Mémorial
pour ses magnifiques Nymphæas Hybrides

✳ ✳ ✳

Adresse télégraphique :

Latour, Temple-sur-Lot

✳ ✳ ✳

VILLENEUVE-SUR-LOT
IMPRIMERIE RENAUD LEYGUES
19, COURS VICTOR-HUGO, 19

'Rocky Stream Garden and Lily Pool, by Messrs Veitch of Exeter' was used as an illustration by Gertrude Jekyll in *Wall and Water Gardens* (1901). The Devon nursery was run by Robert Veitch, who worked in close collaboration with Killerton House. In the early 1900s William Robinson designed their herbaceous borders.

Carnea', 4 *N*. 'Marliacea Chromatella', 3 *N*. 'Marliacea Rosea', 3 *N*. 'Odorata Alba', 8 x *N*. 'Odorata Rosacea', 6 *N. odorata rubra* (Cape Cod), 3 *N*. 'Odorata Sulphurea', and 1 *N*. 'Pygmaea Alba' were despatched. He regrets that the *N*. 'Odorata Exquisita' were still too weak to send but should be ready within the week. In June Saumarez ordered one each of *N*. 'Laydekeri fulgens' and *N*. 'Seignoureti' at

150 francs. These would have been the water lilies which inspired William Robinson.

A bamboo specialist and botanist, A.B. Freeman-Mitford's horticultural skills had developed when the Royal Parks had come under his remit. In his autobiography *Memories*, he described how he had laid out the Dell at the lower end of the Serpentine in Hyde Park 'as a sub-tropical garden with palms, tree ferns, dracaenas and other beauties, planted the little stream with water-lilies, royal fern and so forth, and made it from an eyesore and a den of horrors into what it now is'. He landscaped his estate at Batsford in Gloucestershire which has many springs and streams, with Japanese and Chinese trees and bamboos. After regular exchanges, Latour-Marliac was delighted to learn that he planned to visit Le Temple with Robinson in 1896. However, in the event, he was less than pleased to learn that Mitford was unable to make the journey.

The Jekyll Connection

In celebration of Queen Victoria's Diamond Jubilee in 1897, the Royal Horticultural Society created the Victoria Medal of Honour (VMH) 'in perpetual remembrance of Her Majesty's glorious reign and to enable the Council to confer honour on British horticulturists'. Sixty medals were presented on 26th October and ten of the recipients' names appear in the archives: Gertrude Jekyll, James Hudson, F.W. Burbidge, Rev. Canon Henry Nicholson Ellacombe, Dean Samuel Reynolds Hole, Edwin Molyneux, George Nicholson, Ellen Willmott, and nurserymen Peter Barr and William Bull. Thanks to William Robinson the British were Latour-Marliac's best customers, more than the French or Americans.

Gertrude Jekyll was a good friend of Robinson. In 1883 she had been given fifteen acres to create a garden, Munstead Wood near Godalming in Surrey, her house designed by Edwin Lutyens was completed in 1897. Both her personal and their joint commissions invariably included a water lily pool. In

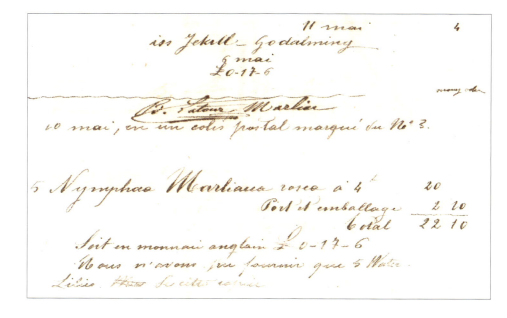

May 1904 Jekyll ordered five *Nymphaea* 'Marliacea Rosea'

Orders for Gertrude Jekyll and Monet were dispatched within two weeks of each other in May 1904. Jekyll's was for a modest five *Nymphaea* 'Marliacea Rosea'.

The planting details do not include which varieties of water lilies she recommends for the lily tanks in the extensive Rose Garden at Highmount, Guildford, Surrey. In the text she summarised: 'Four ways, twelve feet wide, with groups of steps and partly sloping, lead to the lower grassy level, where a large octagonal tank with a wide stone kerb has groups of many coloured water lilies. … sections that are in full blaze of the noonday and early afternoon sun are of strong, warm colouring, for the most part orange and scarlet: the colour-scheme working round both ways to the cool and tender tints that are more acceptable on the shadier sides.'

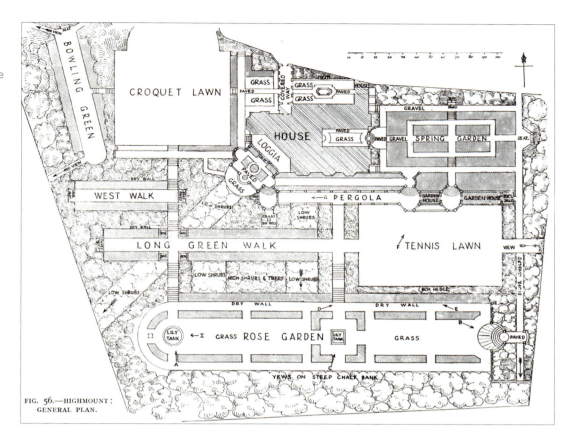

FIG. 56.—HIGHMOUNT: GENERAL PLAN.

Jekyll's book *Home and Garden* (1900) she enthused about 'the eminent French horticulturist, M Latour-Marliac'. Jekyll also entered the Latour-Marliac archives in 1900 when she was co-editing *The Garden* magazine founded by Robinson, they were interested in featuring and illustrating his new varieties. In the same letter, quoted at length under 'The Elusive Blue' (page 124) we get one of the clearest insights into the vexed question of breeding hardy blue water lilies. Latour-Marliac sent her 'a flower of the beautiful hardy *Nymphaea* 'Atropurpurea', blood-red and very dark, the shining petals pointing into a cowl at their extremity.' In May 1904 Jekyll ordered five *N.* 'Marliacea Rosea' at 4 francs. They were only in direct touch again in 1906 although her good friendship with Robinson continued until her death in 1932.

Jekyll's first books *Wood and Garden* (1899) and *Home and Garden* (1900) were written very much in the context of her gardens at Munstead Wood which included a small lily tank. She promised to write more about the new water lilies from Latour-Marliac. This she did in *Wall and Water Gardens* (1901) already much quoted. *Gardens for Small Country Houses* (1912) was a larger book that was co-authored with Sir Lawrence Weaver, it included many garden plans and her own excellent photographs. Many of the plans included a lily tank such as this one for Westbrook in Godalming, Surrey.

Rule Britannia

Cornwall's mild climate fostered the development of new and exotic plant introductions. One noted collector was John Charles Williams of Caerhays Castle, who devoted his life to the cultivation and study of Chinese flora and, like Latour-Marliac, was also closely involved with local affairs. The Williams family had rescued the estate, were plant hunters and breeders of camellias, rhododendrons, magnolias and daffodils; their wealth was derived from tin and copper mines around Redruth. The first orders during 1894 and 1895 were for bamboos and *Nymphaea*. Apart from bamboos and, in 1896 *Nelumbium*, whose despatch was delayed by a rigorous frost, Latour-Marliac sent descriptions and prices of his 'very hardy and available' *Nymphaea*. Williams duly selected 'Ellisiana', 'Marliacea Rubra Punctata' and 'Gloriosa'. Another Cornish customer was Jonathon Rashleigh of Menabilly who ordered bamboos in 1894 and 1895, a few decades later his property became the Cornish home of the author Daphne du Maurier.

In 1898 Jeremiah Colman, scion of the mustard family (who claimed that their fortune had been made from what people left on the side of their plates), heard the paper Latour-Marliac prepared for the Royal Horticultural Society. Colman had bought the Gatton Park estate near Reigate in Surrey in 1888, its hallmark sinuous lake fed by two smaller ponds and a serpentine stream that had been created by the English landscaper Lancelot 'Capability' Brown in the 1760s. H.E. Milner (another VMH recipient) had improved the historic plan and added a series of gardens.

On 20th February 1899 Latour-Marliac wrote with delight regarding the previous year and offering his advice on creating a *plantation* of water lilies enclosing his catalogue with prices.

On 7th May 1904 ninety-one water lilies were despatched. Ten years after this Colman employed a large group of locally unemployed men to create a Japanese garden. Amongst English nurseries used by Colman was V.N. Gauntlett & Co. Limited, an important Latour-Marliac commercial customer. Colman was an enthusiastic collector of orchids, decades later he privately published *Hybridisation of Orchids: The Experience of an Amateur* – he would have recognised a kindred spirit in Latour-Marliac.

Botanical Customers

Latour-Marliac was in contact with the Royal Botanic Gardens, Kew from his first hybridisations. F.W. Burbidge,

'Directeur de Royal Botanic Gardens, Glasnevin, Dublin' appears in 1889, Latour-Marliac mentions his association with Robinson as well as the Duke of Leinster '… and other great notables [who] like my water lilies …' It seems likely that Burbidge visited the *Exposition Universelle* in 1889.

Burbidge was a nineteenth century polymath – gardener, botanist, artist, plant-collector and author – he trained with the Horticultural Society at Chiswick and then worked at Kew. He had associations both with Robinson, for whom he worked at *The Garden*, and Peter Veitch, whose family nursery were excellent Latour-Marliac customers for decades. Burbidge ordered annually between 1889 and 1894, then again in 1904.

Global Gardeners

One of the primary sources of *Nymphaea* for Latour-Marliac's hybridisation programmes was North America where he built up an exchange with several growers. Many of his hybrids were represented at the Columbian World Exposition 1893 and in Chicago parks thereafter. One well-known name on the customer list was Frederick Olmsted operating from Brookline, Massachusetts. Several orders during 1891 and 1892 were for the Vanderbilts at Biltmore in South Carolina for whom Olmsted was landscaping. On 5th February 1892 500 bamboos had been sent to them. More bamboos were ordered in March, followed by a large quantity of bamboos and aquatics in April. Orders continued in 1893, but that year on 4th July Latour-Marliac wrote to Olmsted regarding the very irritating difficulties with the U.S. Government legislation over the delivery of packages and payment. This was to prove an ongoing problem so that eventually Latour-Marliac hybrids were only sent via American nurseries.

The flora of the waters spreads

Orders were sent across Europe and into Russia, shipments were made to East and West Coast America and to Australia including a large order to the Centennial Park, Sydney in 1906. Thomas W. Pockett, Victoria, has several entries leading up to a final note on 18th October 1907: 'I have indeed received your order of 20th August, but I cannot follow it up owing to the fact that the importation of plants is strictly forbidden throughout Australia. With all my regrets, please agree to my sincere greetings.'

Latour-Marliac's stated ambition to spread his enthusiasm was fulfilled beyond his wildest dreams and more than matched by his courtesy, efficiency and outstanding knowledge.

Facing page: The collecting and hybridising of tropical water lilies undertaken by Louis Van Houtte was inspirational for Latour-Marliac. The nursery appears in the first archive book in 1881 when Latour-Marliac bought *N. lotus*, later in the year he ordered Pistia, Pontederia and Nelumbium seeds.

Nursery to Nursery

Long before Latour-Marliac created his award winning exhibit at the *Exposition Universelle* in 1889, he had created a global network of nurseries with whom he exchanged a range of plants and ideas. Many of the entries for 1881 relate to buying and selling bamboos, however, there are nurseries that will appear on the books for the next 43 years, not only regarding orders despatched but also requests for stock – names such as the famous Louis Van Houtte nursery, Gand (Ghent) in Belgium. A brisk trade continued throughout his and his son's lifetime and continued with the Laydekers. Two further nurseries that appear regularly from 1881 are Lagrange at Oullin and Haage et Schmidt at Erfurt. In the ensuing decades the advantages of large orders were outweighed by some unscrupulous nurseries renaming or claiming Marliac hybrids as their own.

Nursery catalogues were a key part in increasing sales, a fact Latour-Marliac made full use of by incorporating elegant descriptions of each plant. In England, Peter Barr and James Veitch were amongst the first with illustrated catalogues dating back to 1862. All this extra information unsurprisingly also offered the opportunity for enhancing the product. The *Gardeners' Chronicle* attacked inaccuracies and even suggested plant descriptions were unnecessary in what was effectively a stock list for the trade. A regular English customer of Latour-Marliac's who ordered copious amounts, H. Cannell and Sons, Swanley, Kent assured his customers in an 1895 *Gardeners' Chronicle*:

> '… our new and complete CATALOGUE … remembering it does not contain a host of enthusiastic sensations that never come to pass, but such as may be thoroughly relied upon …'

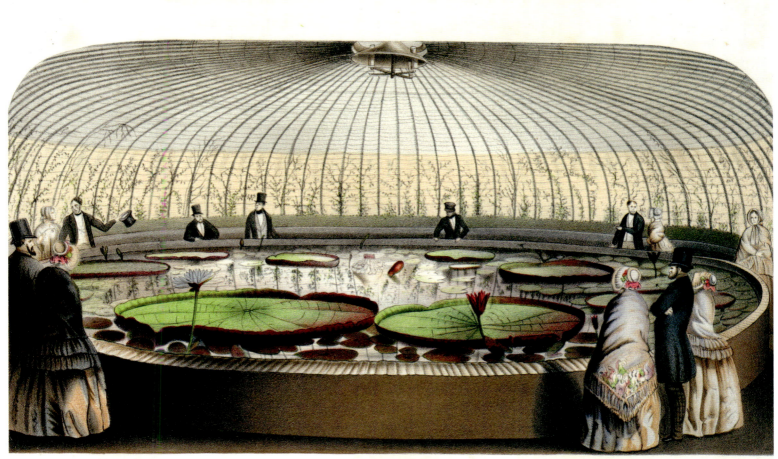

Off. Lith. & pict. in Horto van Houtteans

Vue intérieure de la SERRE VICTORIA *, dans l'Etablissement* Van Houtte

VII, 654-5 ½

Friends and Nurserymen

Seedsman Maurice Andrieux de Vilmorin and Alexandre Godefroy-Lebeuf were key horticultural contacts with whom Latour-Marliac enjoyed long and fruitful relationships.

The first archive entry pertaining to Vilmorin was on 3rd March 1881 when Latour-Marliac sent 20 francs to Monsieur Vilmorin-Andrieux et Cie, Paris in payment for the plants sent on 19th February. Orders and correspondence continued until 1909. Vilmorin was also in touch with William Robinson who had in 1885 published and translated Vilmorin's book *The Vegetable Garden – Illustrations, Descriptions, and Culture of the Garden Vegetables of Cold and Temperate Climates*.

The name Godefroy-Lebeuf appears in many contexts, not least as founder of the bi-monthly *Le Jardin* in 1887, his involvement in both *Expositions Universelles* and his friendship with Monet. He lived in Argenteuil where he had his nursery, to which Latour-Marliac addressed all his correspondence except during the *Expositions*. The seedsman side of the business operated from Paris which Godefroy-Lebeuf used as his base when working at the *Expositions*. They exchanged many different plants and ideas up until his death in 1903, and most of Latour-Marliac's water lily novelties were first profiled in *Le Jardin*. His professional speciality in the family nurseries was building up colonial plants to commercial quantities e.g. *Hevea* (rubber). He used these contacts as introductions for Édgard Latour-Marliac when he travelled out to French Indochina and with the Saigon Botanic Garden for Latour-Marliac père. He was a harsh critic of the state of Paris's *Jardin des Plantes*, campaigned for green spaces in Paris and was an early exponent of the importance of plant diversity. In short, a passion for the development and improvement of plants that both men shared, courses through their correspondence.

Their exchanges bemoan the paucity of literature on aquatics, this would be remedied by regular articles by both of them over the ensuing years in *Le Jardin* and elsewhere.

Wholesale quantities

Nurseries around the world began to trade with Latour-Marliac. In America, these included Edmund D Sturtevant, and the Philadelphia Press in 1882 declared that he possessed 'the rarest and complete collection of Water Lilies ever witnessed in this country'. Trade was both ways with Latour-Marliac ordering from Sturevant's nursery and Latour-Marliac sending out his new varieties. Henry A. Dreer Nurseries which is now defunct, was another loyal customer as was William Tricker. America's oldest water garden specialist, established in 1892, which is still active today.

In the UK, spurred on by the writings of Gertrude Jekyll and William Robinson, nurseries including Veitch of Exeter and Chelsea, which was arguably the most famous nursery on Latour-Marliac's books, and William Bull on the King's Road in Chelsea both put in large orders for water lilies. William Bull sold them from vast glass houses to protect them from pollution – rather than the weather. The nursery James Backhouse & Son of York was associated with the brick pools for water lilies at Burnby Hall Gardens which now holds the national collection of hardy water lilies. H Cannell and Sons in Swanley was one of the first English nurseries to place an order in June 1888 and Dickson's of Chester followed in the next year having, it would appear, found Latour-Marliac at the *Exposition Universelle*. Lakeland nurseries in Windermere, Paul & Son of Cheshunt and one of Jekyll's favoured nurseries V.N. Gaurlett had ordered large quantities, as did Kelways of Langport, Somerset and Wallace & Company of Colchester, Essex.

Amos Perry – whose tenure at Perry's Hardy Plant Farm at Enfield, Middlesex earned him a worldwide reputation and the Victoria Medal of Honour from the Royal Horticultural Society in 1935 – became a longstanding and difficult customer. His first order was placed on 18th April 1899 and his orders continued until the outbreak of the Second World War.

In France, Antoine Lagrange ordered many water lilies

An illustration on 'Water Gardening' from what Perry called his 'book catalogue' c.1922. It was indeed comprehensive with excellent lists of plants and planting ideas. He opened the section: 'For many years I have paid great attention to "Water Gardening", and there has been a great reaction in this class of plant. There is always a fascination in water and its surroundings. With judgment and careful selection how beautiful our lakes, streams and swamps might be made by covering the surface with foliage and flowers, and the margins beautifully fringed with luxuriant vegetation. The rippling stream, the rushing torrent, or the silent lake, has always a charm, and one never tires of meandering along the margins, admiring nature's grand provision for the adornment of the water as well as for the land.' Or indeed, as illustrated, a half barrel.

Latour-Marliac's trade spread throughout the world from this, his desk in Le Temple-sur-Lot. He kept meticulous records of all of his transactions with commercial and domestic customers.

In the United Kingdom, Burnby Hall acknowledges that the Marliac varieties are the most reliable plants in their National Collection of Hardy Water Lilies because they do not cross with others. Bennett's Water Gardens has 86 varieties on offer of which 46 are Marliac. The Dorset Water Lily Company has 29 of which 27 are Marliac. Sadly the most celebrated nursery, Stapeley Water Gardens which was closely associated with the modern history of Latour-Marliac, closed in January 2012 after being in business for forty-five years.

In Germany where water lily translates into a poetic *seerosen* (sea rose) the legacy of Haage et Schmidt is continued by two major nurseries: Jörg Petrowsky in Eschede offering 117 varieties of which 38 are Marliac: and Nymphaion de Werner Wallner Gartenbaubetrieb, Kirchheim in Schwaben, has 125 of which 55 are Marliac.

Looking at these figures, Robert Sheldon, the current owner, reckons that the average American and European water lily nursery has at least one-third of its stock in Marliac varieties and for about half of these nurseries Marliac varieties represent at least 50 per cent of their stock. Today the bulk of Latour-Marliac SARL's customers are private gardeners and landscapers.

Last Word
Chronique Horticole 19 mai 1911 No 10

'M. *Latour-Marliac* – This excellent horticulturist who has just died, had acquired a universal reputation for the culture of aquatic plants, of which he had introduced numerous and brilliant crosses. In his establishment in Le Temple-sur-Lot (Lot-et-Garonne), M. Latour-Marliac worked for forty years on the hybridisation of Nymphéas, and, after lengthy experiments, he had succeeded in obtaining novelties whose names are known today by all enthusiasts: N. Marliacea chromatella, flammea, rosea, N. atropurpurea, N. colossea, N. odorata exquisita, N. pygmaea Helvola, N. virginalis, N. Ellisiana, etc., etc. These beautiful plants received the highest recognition, in France and abroad, and the *Revue Horticole* has been pleased to alert their readers to them. M. Latour-Marliac, who died at the age of eighty years, was intellectually active until the end. He leaves his wife who was always an active accomplice, to succeed him as head of his establishment, and a son'.

Le Secretaire de la Redaction G.T. Grignan

A Short List of the Named and Famed

'Mons. B. Latour-Marliac, who has brought the lovely colours and forms of the water lilies of the east to the waters of the north, the forty-fourth volume of *The Garden* is dedicated by its founder.
William Robinson, January 1894'.

Out of the thousands of seedlings that Latour-Marliac raised to select eligible novelties, he celebrated those whose work and allegiance he admired by naming a water lily after them as did his son and grandsons after him. It is no exaggeration to say that his most admired and useful contact was William Robinson.

William Robinson

On the advice of his good customer James Saumarez, in 1887 Latour-Marliac wrote to William Robinson to introduce himself:
'Today has been a good one in this regard with the flowering of what appears to be a magnificent *Nymphaea* amongst the innumerable seedlings that I trial every year.

This *Nymphaea* to which I have given the name of *Marliacea chromatella foliis hepatiis marmoralis* is noted for the size of its flowers which measure fifteen centimetres across and by the depth of its leaves, of a distinctly different type. It has absolute hardiness even when in bud, and the flowers remain open during most of he day, offering a mass of blooms from the beginning of May until the end of October. The leaves alone are richly marbled, with reddish brown across their edges and abundantly spotted with russet red... The box I have addressed to you contains:

1. A yellow flower on its first day of opening.
2. A yellow flower whose exterior petals are pink at the base, on its third day of opening and in its full flowering.
3. Two reddish brown marbled leaves under the limb [botanical term for the broadened flattened part] and spotted with red on the under side.

In case you would like to possess other flowers in order to make a display for your own pleasure I will send you other examples'.

Latour-Marliac's timing could not have been better. According to Robinson's *Tree and Garden Book*, a meticulous and opinionated journal of his work on his estate, later published as *Gravetye Manor or Twenty Years' Work round an Old Manor House 1885-1908*, he had just cleared out his lake, having bought Gravetye Manor, near East Grinstead in Sussex three years earlier. In 1871

A contemporary photograph of Robinson's lower lake that he used to illustrate his writings. After a hot day in London Robinson would get his chauffeur to drop him at the far end of the lake so that he could swim its length and walk up to the house refreshed.

Following his great success as a writer and promulgator of the natural garden, in 1884 Robinson bought Gravetye Manor near East Grinstead in Sussex, it dates from the late Elizabethan period. The water lily pool in 2015.

Robinson had founded *The Garden* magazine, which he would continue to edit until 1899. This was the start of a professional and personal friendship that developed into one of great significance and importance to both men. They exchanged plants, presents (books, wine and prunes); Robinson visited on several occasions, became a family friend and Latour-Marliac's greatest ambassador. This firm friendship continued with Édgard Latour-Marliac after his father's death in January 1911.

Robinson's *Tree and Garden Book* in 1892 notes:

'Water-lilies. The first brought here and planted in the Upper Lake were the common white and yellow from Shrubland Park ... Planted also a new hybrid Water-lily, raised in France (*N. Marliacea*), in the same pond.'

In March 1893 Robinson ordered more water lilies, noting:

'New Water-lilies. Planted a large collection of new finely coloured kinds raised in France and sent me by M. Latour-Marliac and M. Maurice de Vilmorin. ... We had great success in the past Summer with these Water-lilies, which flowered till the middle of Autumn, noble buds and flowers being gathered towards the end of October. Some may think that the sunny days of the present year may have been

sufficient to account for this success, but among the many beautiful plants Lord de Saumarez has tried at Shrubland are all the hybrids obtainable of this never-to-be-forgotten raiser ... Most of the new kinds were planted in the Spring of the present year, and in a few months we got very good blooms and red Water-lilies visible at long distances the first year of their growth. ...' The latest varieties would continue to be despatched annually to adorn Gravetye's lakes and pond.

In August 1893 Robinson wrote that he would be dedicating the bound volume of that year's issues of *The Garden* to Latour-Marliac and Robinson commissioned an article from him to describe his work. On 4th March 1894 Latour-Marliac thanked Robinson for *The Garden* of 24th February with its charming coloured plate of *Nymphaea* 'Laydekeri Rosea'. On 21st August 1894 Robinson was sent: 'the most handsome hybrid that I have ever obtained; and I announce to you that I will be sending a postal package to your address tomorrow which contains two flowers of this very hardy beauty of a *N.* that will carry your name'. In fact the highly fertile seed bearing *N.* 'Laydekeri Grandiflora' was crossed with pollen from *N. mexicana* to produce *N.* 'Robinsonii', 'Ellisiana' and 'Seignoureti'.

Nymphaea 'Robinsonii' (1895, Latour-Marliac). As a mark of the bond between them, Latour-Marliac named one of his new hybrids for William Robinson. The very essence of Robinson's robust Irish mind and frame seem embodied in Latour-Marliac's description: 'The N. Robinsonii is excessively hardy and at the time when I will send it to you, it will not need shelter in order to assist its growth; it is a robust *gaillard* (fellow), which does not need to be treated like an invalid and which asks only for open air'.

1895 dawned with Latour-Marliac's offer of some exciting samples including: 'The *N*. Robinsonii … excessively hardy … it will not need shelter … it is a robust *gaillard* (fellow). Meanwhile, during that summer and autumn, four artists captured the garden scene unfolding at Gravetye: Mark Fisher, Alfred Parsons, H.A. Olivier and H.G. Moon.

During 1896 Robinson's garden journal records his plans to visit Latour-Marliac that year, which he successfully repeated in 1898. An insight into their friendship is gained on 27th October when Latour-Marliac wrote thanking him for 'the pretty books you have sent me for my young family which have been enthusiastically received'. In return he sent some 'Agen prunes [which] are delicious, wrinkled but not dry' – a comment equally relevant today. On 27th December Latour-Marliac 'couldn't let 1899 be in sight without greeting you' and sending 24 bottles of white wine.

During 1899 Robinson sent some varieties such as *N*. 'Marliacea Rosea' to Latour-Marliac, presumably from another source or possibly seedlings from the parent plant. Latour-Marliac provided three examples of *N*. 'Odorata Sulphurea Grandiflora' plus three novelties.

In May we get a glimpse of the hot weather prior to the 1900 *Exposition Universelle* and the year closed with a general discussion on using Colza oil to get rid of pernicious insects and a salutation from Latour-Marliac: '…At the dawn of a new century I raise a warm witness to your work'.

Robinson noted in his *Tree and Garden Book* that he had cleared the Lower Lake. In February Latour-Marliac wrote that he was pleased to learn that he wanted an assortment of water lilies as well as the thought of all the visitors at Gravetye seeing his water lilies.

Two years elapsed until 29th November 1904 when Latour-Marliac wrote describing his attack of paralysis in 1902, before unsurprisingly moving on to the subject of a new water lily – 'Paul Hariot'.

Although Latour-Marliac's health had been tried by the rigours of the winter, the correspondence was back to normal in 1905. On 5th February he recommended a selection of red flowers whilst Robinson sent him a copy of *Flora and Sylva* including an engraving of *N*. 'Colossea'. He pointed out the new 'Paul Hariot', and that 'Vésuve' (now very rare) had the most beautiful red flowers.

The last non routine exchange was on 22nd September 1905, there were only three letters plus advertisements placed in *Gardening Illustrated* which were now signed C. Laydeker from 1906 until 1909. In an article on his ponds in *Country Life* of March 6, 1909 Robinson wrote: 'It is worth noting that we have four sources of supply for our water planting – trees …, shrubs …; water-side plants … and true water plants like the Water-lily. These of late years give the crowning charm to the water itself; their beauty of colour is extraordinary, and they are almost worth growing for the sake of the foliage alone.

Their hardiness in our climate is remarkable. Some groups have been eighteen years in one place, and though never touched or attended to in any way, have improved every year. … But while they grow anywhere, one can never enjoy their full beauty unless some enemies are kept down. Chief among them are the water-vole and the water hen …'

Latour-Marliac died in January 1911. The next letter to Robinson was dated 3rd March 1912 from Édgard and included… 'please believe my feelings towards you will be just the same as my father's. I thank you very much for the article about Nymphaea 'Sioux' in *Gardening Illustrated* 2 March'

Correspondence slowed but didn't cease due to the war and the last Robinson entry in the archives was in April 1920 – a complimentary N. 'Meteor'.

The Honourable Charles Ellis

Charles Ellis was a traveller and naturalist who bought Frensham Hall and its farms at Shottermill near Haslemere in Surrey in 1894. Latour-Marliac first mentions his name on 5th April and the correspondence became fairly frequent and at times lengthy during 1894 and 1895. On 24th March 1896 Latour-Marliac acknowledged an enquiry for *Nymphcea* including the new and expensive N. 'Seignoureti' and N.

'Aurora' at 100 francs a piece which were duly despatched. He noted with pleasure that Ellis had seen the splendid yellow water lilies that Lord de Saumarez was growing, which he suggested were probably N. 'Odorata Sulphurea Grandiflora'. Ellis sent further large water lily and aquatics orders in April and May, running up a bill of 2,091,60 F (£82/19/11). He introduced Lord Kesteven and confirmed that he planned to make the journey to Le Temple-sur-Lot. On 8th July Latour-Marliac thanked Ellis for his grateful letter following the successful visit. He confirmed that he would be in touch regarding his 1897 spring novelties such as N. 'Ellisiana' , N. 'Gloriosa', N. 'Andréana', and N. 'Marliacea Rubra Punctata' – not only would Ellis have first refusal but he was also invited to choose 'his' *Nymphaea*. From which one can conclude when he visited and saw it, he was pleased with his namesake as was Latour-Marliac.

Ellis died at Frensham Hall in 1906 aged 66. Two years later the named and famed gardener Mrs Richmond selected the N. 'Ellisiana' as: 'one of the most brilliant in colour, being almost vermilion in tint', her descriptions *In My Lady's Garden* continued to enthuse about the next namesake, N. 'Paul Hariot'; '… the blossoms … are in pale pink flushed with carmine in the centre, like those of a blush-rose'.

Nymphaea 'Ellisiana' (1896, Latour-Marliac). Named for The Honorable Charles Ellis, who visited Le Temple-sur-Lot in July 1897. From Latour-Marliac's letters to him afterwards it can be assumed that he was shown the water lily that would carry his name – 'Ellisiana'. The pomegranate red flowers with lively orange stamens are suitable for smaller garden ponds.

Paul Hariot

Paul Hariot was a botanical artist best known for illustrating the sumptuous *Le Livre d'Or des Roses* (The Golden Book of Roses) which was published in 1885 when he was 29. The roses he painted were those that were grown in French gardens at the time. His influence was such that in 1902, the Lemoine nursery introduced a rose named 'Paul Hariot' with deep purple-lilac double flowers. In a 1905 letter from Latour-Marliac to Paul Hariot in Paris:

'In accordance with your request I am enclosing under the same cover, my aquatic plants catalogue in which you will find mention of the Nymphaea to which you have been kind enough to give your name. The examples that I have are still underdeveloped, but I will happily put one at your disposition if that is what you would like'.

The *Nymphaea* 'Paul Hariot' proved very popular and continues to be so today.

Mrs Richmond

'Hardy water-lilies in many shades of crimson, yellow, pink, and white, are easily grown in tubs, sunk to the rim in the soil or the sward. These fine hybrid *Nymphaeas* are too easily choked by coarser plants in a lake, and should be grown separately.'
Mrs I.L. Richmond, *In My Lady's Garden* 1908

Mrs Richmond was the Editor of *The Queen* magazine from 1888-1898, and her editorship was particularly noted for its hand-coloured fashion plates by A. Sandoz. Mrs I.L. Richmond was a Fellow of the Royal Horticultural Society and published several books including a year round collection of writings *In My Lady's Garden* in 1908 illustrated by Beatrice Parsons which included coloured plates of *Nymphaea* 'Lucida' and 'Gloriosa'. The deep pink flowering *N.* 'Mrs Richmond' was introduced in 1910.

After Latour-Marliac's death Édgard reported to Mrs Richmond on a blue *Nymphaea* that had survived the relatively mild winter of 1911/12 in the open air, unsheltered and in water that was not from the thermal spring-water. If it carried on he would send some for her to trial. Like his father he was keeping the family's best interests to the fore.

Mrs Richmond, or rather Mr, was then instrumental in finding somewhere for Édgard's nephew to stay in England and Mrs Richmond subsequently kept the family posted as to Camille Laydeker's progress.

Facing page: *Nymphaea* 'Paul Hariot' (1905, Latour-Marliac). A personal acknowledgement for the botanical artist to whom Latour-Marliac sent the first flowers and leaves. Hariot was celebrated for painting roses growing in French gardens, the subject of *The Golden Book of Roses* (1885). It was an immensely popular water lily and remains a favourite. A large water lily suitable for pools and small lakes. Hariot and Latour-Marliac also corresponded about tulips and onions.

Right: *Nymphaea* 'Mrs Richmond' (1910, Latour-Marliac). *The Journal of the Royal Horticultural Society* reported that the judges were unanimous in their award on 29th August 1911 'To *N.* 'Mrs Richmond' A rose-pink of great beauty. The flowers which measure 8 inches across, are of good shape, and have a mass of golden-yellow stamens in the middle. The foliage is of medium size, and very dark green in colour'.

James Hudson

The exemplary roots of James Hudson's career went deep, in no small part because his father had been Head Gardener at Horsted Place in Sussex. While working in a private garden, Deepdene in Dorking, Surrey, Hudson sat a new examination in horticulture in London and achieved full marks, a record unbeaten some 40 years later. In 1876 Hudson was appointed Head Gardener at Gunnersbury Park, West London, by J.H. Atkinson. He continued under Leopold de Rothschild when he acquired the estate in 1889 and finally rejoined Gunnersbury Park with Gunnersbury House. He held this post until his retirement in 1919. Hudson and Gunnersbury became synonymous with gardening of the highest standard. He was held in excellent esteem as an exhibitor at shows, a landscaper and plant breeder. Contemporary magazines regularly profiled his talent for producing large quantities of fruit, vegetables and flowers. He also contributed to the *Journal of the Royal Horticultural Society, Gardeners' Chronicle* and *Country Life*. His landscaping tastes were akin to the wild and natural styles advocated by William Robinson, with whom he became friendly.

Hudson first appeared in the archives on 22nd April 1894 and by the start of the twentieth century, he had become a noted water lily grower in Britain for which he had developed the eastern part of Horseshoe Lake in Gunnersbury Park.

Orders went back and forth until 8th March 1911 when Édgard confirmed his delight that Hudson was planning to visit. This was six weeks after Latour-Marliac's death and *The Garden* approached Hudson to write his obituary. Hudson was welcomed that summer by Édgard and his mother, Alida and, following in his father's tradition, Édgard wrote to him to ask among other things whether he would give his name to one of his 1912 introductions. On 2nd March 1912 *Gardening Illustrated* ran a short article on N. 'James Hudson'.

Facing page: *Nymphaea* 'James Hudson' (1912, Latour-Marliac). This lily with large magnificent tulipiform pink blossoms was named for Leopold de Rothschild's consummately talented Head Gardener. A contemporary account of the Japanese Garden he created at Gunnersbury House recorded: 'Waterlilies of various species, Chinese Palms and Bamboo, and surrounding the whole, a neatly constructed fence of Bamboo rods put together without nails. The country has been ransacked by Mr. Hudson, the gardener, for plants of Chinese or Japanese origin wherewith to give suitable realistic effects'. The lily is large, free flowering and suitable for ponds and pools.

Right: The fruits of James Hudson's labours admired by Leopold de Rothschild wearing a straw boater and leaning on a walking cane beside the lily pond at Gunnersbury Park. The blurred image at his feet is the family dog.

Below: *Nymphaea* 'Marguerite Laplace' (1913, Latour-Marliac). Édgard celebrated the good relations between him and Monsieur Laplace by naming his water lily with large pink flowers that fade to white for his wife.

Marguerite Laplace

Monsieur Laplace, whose first name remains a mystery, was actively involved on the French horticultural scene and the redesigning of the Bagatelle gardens, not least with another dedicatee, J.C.N. Forestier. Laplace enters the archives on 17th August 1912 when Édgard sent him the flowers and leaves of the new 'Goliath' for which he requested a detailed description as it was the first time it had been in circulation. Later that year he wrote to say that they would like to name a new water lily *N.* 'Marguerite Laplace' in honour of his wife. Following chronic bronchitis and pulmonary congestion, Édgard wrote again on 20th October to congratulate him on an article in *Le Jardin* of 5th October and to invite him to stay the following July or August. Laplace took up the offer.

When Édgard despatched the first flowers of the new *N.* 'Marguerite Laplace' he reassured the family that they were small because he had only split the stock in November, given time the flowers would be as beautiful as *N.* 'Newton', 'Escarboucle', and 'Meteor'.

J.C.N. Forestier

Forestier, Conservateur des Promenades de la Ville de Paris, Bois de Boulogne, appears from 1913 in the archives, both personally and in relation to his international work. He had strongly advocated the purchase of the Parc de Bagatelle for the city of Paris in 1904, following which he was instrumental in making it one of Paris' loveliest parks, not least Forestier acknowledged Monet's influence in the rose gardens. Édgard ensured that the sinuous eighteenth-century lake was a showcase for water lilies 'they must all be presented as the collection of M. Latour-Marliac with this rejoinder: that M. Latour-Marliac was the hybridiser of one or another, when this would be the case.'

Forestier designed parks throughout Europe and beyond in Latin America and Morocco and remained a good customer. In 1929 the Laydekers introduced the *N.* 'J.C.N. Forestier' in celebration of his work as a landscape architect.

Nymphaea 'J.C.N. Forestier' (1929, Latour-Marliac). Forestier was an influential landscape architect who amongst many projects, turned *parc de Bagatelle* into one of Paris' loveliest parks. He was a customer over many years and ordered water lilies from Édgard Latour-Marliac for the lakes at the Bagatelle during the 1920s. The alliance was marked around 1930 when the Laydekers introduced this tall-stemmed apricot water lily.

The Lyon connection – René Gerard

Many of France's newer *jardins botaniques* date from a decree issued in 1794 which required all towns with a population of over 300,000 to establish a school (*polytechnique*) that taught science literature and arts with a botanical garden. Lyon was one such city and its *Jardin botanique du Parc de la Tête d'Or* had been used by the city to host a universal, international and colonial *Exposition*.

Once more Édgard continued the tradition of naming good customers when on 25th October 1913 he wrote thanking M Gérard, *Professeur à la Faculé des Sciences* in Lyon for agreeing to have a water lily named for him. Édgard asked that the description of *Nymphaea* 'René Gérard' should not be divulged. Gérard created a *bassin* in the parc especially for this water lily and others from the Latour-Marliac stable. Édgard later noted that 'Rene Gérard' appeared in almost all the overseas main catalogues: Dreer mentioned it in America and Larsen in his catalogue in Copenhagen.

And Julien Chifflot

Julien Chifflot is described as Doctor of Natural Sciences, Graduate of Physical Sciences and Head of Botanical Works in the Faculty of Sciences, Lyon, and Deputy Director of the town's Botanical Garden. Amongst many other honours he was also the Vice-President of the *Société lyonnaise d'horticulture*. He was the expert witness in November 1913 for Édgard's lengthy court case which proved that rival

Nymphaea 'René Gérard' (1914, Latour-Marliac). Édgard described it thus: 't is a vigorous variety that will develop rapidly. It has ample leaves, disc shaped with open wavy margins and strongly pointed lobes, they are lightly indented on the upper side; dark green on both surfaces; the underside is often nuanced with crimson or purple. The flowers are full, very large (25-30cm/10-12in or more in diameter) and have elongated sepals, lanceolated, muddy purple without and pink within; long petioles, pale pink ovules, variegated and striped with pinkish crimson; the shades and the stripes are accentuated as much by the petioles which are close to the centre of the flower, in such a way that the most central have a vivid pinkish-crimson, put into relief by the neighbouring intense ochre-yellow stamens.'

Right: *Nymphaea* 'Madame Julien Chifflot' (1921, Latour-Marliac). In the words of Latour-Marliac's 1921 catalogue: 'The flower's ensemble is of a very beautiful effect set against the green of the leaves, in all a remarkably elite plant' That year three separate pages were dedicated to describing 'Madame Julien Chifflot', 'Souvenir de Jules Jaquier', both retailing at 100 francs, and 'Amabilis' at 80 francs.

Below: *Nymphaea* 'Charles de Meurville' (1931, Latour-Marliac). The man and his flower are encapsulated in the contemporary catalogue description : 'star shaped, pink red darkening at the centre, paling to pink along its edges with orange stamens. Its delicacy is in the image of the perfect elegant man, of high repute and goodness without equal'.

nurseryman Lagrange had tampered with one of Latour-Marliac's lilies and tried to pass it off as his own.

Eight years elapsed until, amongst the three 'Dernières Nouveautés' of the 1921 catalogue each with a page dedicated to their descriptions, *N.* 'Madame Julien Chifflot' made her debut at 100 francs. The numerous petals were finely veined and marked with a carmine red deepening at the base on a pink flower, darkening as it aged.

Charles de Meurville

Charles de Meurville, known as Charles Petit de Meurville, was born on 12th September 1841 in Lyon. His final apartment in Bordeaux was a collector's treasure trove which included paintings, ceramics, bronzes, tapestries, furniture and dolls. He was also an avid collector of eighteenth century engravings. In 1895 he was commissioned to organise a retrospective of Old Masters and Modern Paintings for the *Exposition Internationale de Bordeaux* – surely seen by the Latour-Marliac family? He was a member of almost all the learned societies in Bordeaux where he may well have known or been known by Latour-Marliac and the Laydekers. On his death in 1927 he made considerable donations to Bordeaux's museums. In 1931 Jean Laydeker dedicated a large sprawling vermilion pink blooming water lily to Charles de Meurville.

The Family after Bory

'I offer you, Miss Dobson, a refuge more glorious and more augustly gilded than you ... There is a Jacobean garden of white roses. Between the ends of two pleached alleys, under a dome of branches, is a little lake, with a Triton of black marble, and with water-lilies. Hither and thither under the archipelago of water-lilies, dart gold-fish - tongues of flame in the dark water'. Max Beerbohm Zuleika Dobson, 1911

After Bory's death in January 1911, the name Latour-Marliac and its association with water lilies lived on with his son Édgard. Throughout the bound 1881-1924 archives there is a great deal of correspondence from Bory Latour-Marliac with both his children, Angèle and Édgard, as well as his son-in-law Maurice Laydeker – a clear indication that the whole family took an active interest in the business. A tradition that was continued by Édgard albeit more cantankerously, his irritations mirrored in his increasingly wild, indecipherable handwriting.

Previous page: Here willow frames the view to the ponds where the sun is gleaming on the lily pads. Today the emphasis on the site is as much on enjoying the visual pleasures of aquatic plants as growing them.

Facing page, top: Établissement Latour-Marliac under Édgard: the small tree has no leaves but the surrounding orchard trees do, so this and the somewhat weedy scene suggest that it is probably the end of the season. The shutters on the villa [built 1913] are closed, the terracotta dishes are drained and the grass around the pools looks very overgrown. One person seems to be holding a large box next to the prune drying oven – there appear to be seven adults and seven children

Facing page, bottom: Lake at Parc de Bagatelle, Paris. On 10th August 1922, Édgard Latour-Marliac wrote to J.C.N. Forestier, Conservateur des Promenades de la Ville de Paris, Bois de Boulogne:

'As regards my plants that are displayed at Bagatelle, if I have understood correctly they must all (raised or not raised by me), be presented as the collection of M Latour-Marliac with this rejoinder: that M Latour-Marliac was the hybridiser of one or another, when this would be the case.'

Many unnamed new hybrids were still growing on the nursery so the annual offerings of *nouveautés* continued. Although the family maintained the big house in Le Temple-sur-Lot, the nursery was increasingly wholesale and run remotely from Bordeaux. Apart from closure during World War Two, the nursery remained largely unchanged until Ray and Barbara Davies took over in 1991. They started to renovate the original nursery parts but their greatest legacy is the large lake and its surrounding landscape. The Davies tenure ties in with the popular restoration of Monet's garden at Giverny and the wider public appeal of water lilies on and off the canvas. Since Robert Sheldon bought the nursery in 2007, he has seen a resurgence in retail interest and the desire to visit the source, in every sense, of hardy water lilies.

The Forgotten Latour-Marliac

History has not been kind to Édgard, plenty of condemnation, laced with hints of idleness and extravagance, and an assurance that he had never been involved in the nursery. Delving into the archives gradually revealed a different picture. In 1884 he was appointed *Agent des Postes* for Cochinchine (a region of Indochina that included the Mekong Delta which was a French colony form 1862 to 1954), Latour-Marliac wrote to the Comte de Castillon expressing concern that the climate was not good for Europeans. Writing to Alphonse Karr on 16th February 1884 Latour-Marliac expressed the same worry but adding that Édgard would undoubtedly see some interesting horticultural novelties. Following up an introduction by Godefroy-Lebeuf, Latour-Marliac wrote a letter to the Director o the Saigon Botanic Garden for Édgard to present with two bamboo varieties. He wanted to exchange bamboos, noting that he was the proud possessor of over 50 varieties. Latour-Marliac kept Godefroy-Lebeuf and Castillon apprised of his son's travels.

On 15th January 1911 his father wrote him a lengthy letter, closing: 'And therefore goodbye for now; … in the meantime, I renew with you all the good wishes that I have expressed to you on behalf of your mother and me'. Eleven days later he was dead. Bory's wife Alida continued to live in the main house where Édgard eventually joined her. Although Camille had been helping his grandfather, Édgard started to sign the correspondence the day after his father's death. The 1911 catalogues were mailed and the season appeared to run as usual until October when Angèle (and Maurice) wrote to apologise for the behaviour of Camille who had been deemed unfit to run the nursery. The firm friendships established with his father continued with, amongst many, William Robinson, Mrs Richmond and James Hudson.

When severely debilitated by his ongoing liver complaint, Édgard blamed it on his years in Indochina. Was it the then endemic Hepatitis B? The archives show his handwriting and his mood swings deteriorating dramatically.

American connections

Despite the difficulties over import legislation and the outbreak of war, business continued between Établissement Latour-Marliac and the United States with essentially the same three nurseries Edward Sturtevant, William Tricker and Henry Dreer. On 11th November 1913 Édgard had written to Edmund Sturtevant, Hollywood, LA, California, following the report of some casualties with the plants, he pointed out that this was hardly surprising after such a long journey. Sturtevant (and Henry Dreer) went on receiving plants, Sturtevant's Hollywood nursery was taken over by Harry Johnson who then became a regular customer. On 20th September 1916, Édgard sent his condolences to Mr William Tricker, Chestnut Street, Arlington, NJ, on the death of his father before adding that he could not update his prices as plant imports were forbidden. Service resumed with Dreer after the war and a large order appears in the archives on 2nd April, 1921. One of Édgard's last letters was to thank F.S. Allen of the Water Gardens, Los Angéles, California for a letter dated 10th December 1922 which included 'Californian products' for Christmas presents.

In 1924, the year of Édgard's death, the *Nymphaea* 'Mme Wilfron Gonnère' was introduced, a remembrance of his maternal grandmother. His death marked the end of an era — that of the devoted enthusiast combining commercial interests with botanical friendly exchange, also the nursery lost having a dedicated individual at its head — but the legacy lived on in as yet unnamed water lilies.

The Laydekers

'Monsieur le Comte, The negotiations for my daughter's marriage which is about to take place and of which I am delighted to inform you, has slightly delayed this letter. My future son-in-law Maurice Laydeker is a good man, in active service as deputy for the *Compagnie du Midi* and will be named Inspector at the next promotion. His father is an officer in the *Legion d'honneur* and was 'trésorier payeur des finances' at Strasbourg at the time of the siege, he is now retired. Amongst the advantages I find in this alliance is that of trusting my child to a family of Christian and *légitimiste* traditions ...'

B. Latour-Marliac 3rd July 1882
to the Comte de Castillon

The last sentence provides an insight into beliefs that still divided the nation nearly a century after the 1789 French Revolution. Religious and *légitimiste*, the latter Royalist but in its strictest sense, followers adhered to the belief that the king of France must be of direct descent.

By 1924, the year of Edgard's death, Maurice had retired, so he and Angèle were in a position to oversee the estate and nursery where Camille had already taken charge. On 18th January 1924 the new signature 'C. Laydeker Le Directeur' appeared in the archives, he confirmed that the name of the firm and the nature of their business would remain unchanged. Modern typewritten letters and orders were already being used by 1924 including details of *Nymphaea* and *Nelumbium* sent on 15th November to F. Hintermeyer of Plantas y Flores, Buenos Aires. It is a safe assumption that this connection must have been via Forestier who had designed the city's public park and promenade.

A plain covered catalogue was issued in 1925, of which the title page in English announced 'Specialities of Nymphaeas, Nelumb'ums and other Aquatic Plants', and listed prizes from the Universal Exhibition of 1889 to the International Exhibition Lyon 1914 as well as the assurance 'Our Nurseries are controlled by the *Service Phytopathologique* of the French Ministry of Agriculture'.

In 1924 Camille had married Marcelle Glauzel, they

Facing page: *Nymphaea* 'Goliath'. A lengthy court case in 1913 proved that Lagrange had tampered with *Nymphaea* 'Goliath' and tried to introduce it as of his own crossing. Lagrange had to pay damages of 500 francs.

Right: *Nymphaea* 'Madame Julien Chifflot' gently blooming, reaches for the light, reflects in the water and evokes a description of M Chifflot made by his colleague Rene Gerard: 'Horticulture seduced him; he became a fervent practitioner of its art'.

had two children, Bory and Henriette. Six new water lily varieties were introduced during his directorship 'Pumila Rubra' around 1925, 'Maurice Laydeker' in 1927, 'Colonel A.J. Welch' and 'J.C.N. Forestier' in 1929, and 'Charles de Meurville' in 1931. The sixth and final new *Nymphaea* was 'Mme de Bonseigneur' in 1935. On 26th February 1936 Angèle Laydeker died and Jean Laydeker, Camille's brother, bought him out of the business. Now approaching fifty, Jean took on sole responsibility whilst still working in insurance. After his retirement he devoted more time to the nursery up until his death in 1974. In many ways the survival of his grandfather's site and legacy is thanks to Jean. He worked conscientiously to make the business commercially viable, and he probably built many of the rectangular culture ponds from which he raised and despatched wholesale quantities of the unique Latour-Marliac varieties.

In contrast with his more severe and taciturn character, his wife, Marguerite de la Myre Mory, was warm and talkative. They had two sons, Philippe, born in 1931 and Henri, born in 1933. Later, as well as following full time occupations in

Bordeaux, they also took an active interest in the nursery. Although most correspondence was typed, Jean's immensely tidy, tiny handwritten records and notes would fascinate a graphologist. He was made an Honorary Member of the Association des Fleuristes de France.

Business was almost entirely by mail order and correspondence was directed through Établissements Latour-Marliac, 8 Rue Blanc Dutrouilh, Bordeaux. During 1936 four new water lilies were introduced Bory de St. Vincent', 'Jean de Lamarsalle', 'Mme Bory Latour-Marliac' and 'Mme Maurice Laydeker'. It was also a year for the great and the good. On 6th April an order was placed for lotus on behalf of the Pope from Castel Gandolfo, and on 2nd May *Nelumbium* 'Osiris', 'Flavescens', *speciosum*, *roseum*, 'Album Grandiflorum', and *pekinense rubrum* were despatched. On 30th April a letter on behalf of the King of Bulgaria settled his account of 442,90 francs.

1939 heralded three previously unpublished novelties, a triumvirate of womanhood: 'Princesse Elisabeth' 'cyclamen pink with a central dark red line. Deep pink stamens at the

A view across the lotus pools in summer. In 1936 Pope Pius XI ordered a selection of six *Nelumbium* for his summer palace at Castel Gandolfo. As he enjoyed the sun playing on the double white, pale yellow, rose and deep pink flowers did he meditate on their symbolism?

Édgard introduced 'Indiana' in 1912, this colour illustration from a contemporary magazine shows the flowers on the first, second and third day. It also manages to capture the copper tones and the reflections. Amos Perry, who was a loyal but difficult customer, also stocked *Nymphaea* 'Indiana' describing it as: 'one of the most distinct of the new vars., remarkably free, strong vigorous habit, most conspicuous bright coppery-red leaves. The fls. on opening are a distinct shade of brilliant orange yellow, deepening in colour as the flower ages, on the third and fourth day assuming a most unusual shade of bright copper.'

Nymphaea '**Newton**' was introduced by Édgard who also introduced other new *Nymphaea* 'James Hudson', 'Esmeralda', 'Eucharis', 'Indiana', 'Lusitania', 'Nobilissima', 'Goliath' and 'Tulipiformis'.

Left, top: *Nymphaea* 'Bory de St Vincent'. Jean Laydeker appears to be keen to immortalize the family name beyond Marliacea and Laydekeri. In 1936 as well as 'Mme Maurice Laydeker', he introduced both *Nymphaea* 'Bory de St. Vincent' pictured here, and 'Mme Bory Latour-Marliac'. The former his illustrious great-great uncle and the latter his grandmother.

Left, bottom: *Nymphaea* 'Senegal'. After the First World War Jean Laydeker had lived and worked for many years in Senegal, then part of the French Empire. In 1965 he introduced *Nymphaea* 'Senegal'. In his 1969 leaflet he described it as 'Large flowers, very pretty bright red'. The light here makes it seem more purple than red.

Facing page: The wholesale side of Établissements Latour-Marliac was brought into the twentieth century and commercial efficiency by Jean Laydeker, grandson of Bory Latour-Marliac. The largest rectangular pools seen today were probably built for him as culture ponds to supply a market demanding not tens and hundreds but thousands of water lilies at a time. Between 1936 and 1991 retail business and visitors to the nursery virtually ceased, and all administration was run from Bordeaux.

base, golden yellow at their extremities. Delicious perfume'; 'Mme Maurice Laydeker' 'cherry red self-coloured (globular form)'; and 'Baroness Orczy' 'splendid variety, pink. Very large flowers.' Laydeker sent a round robin to eighteen of his wholesale customers on 21st April: '… each year I await to have finalised the forwarding of my purchaser's requirements … are you going to order or not ….' How could they resist?

Around 1940, although the nursery was closed during the war, three new water lilies were introduced as a patriotic gesture: 'Elisée', 'France', and 'Grésilias'. Laydeker retired from insurance after the Second World War. In 1952 he rented greenhouses near Bordeaux so he could devote more time to the nursery, one new variety was introduced in 1952 'Un Maréchal' – now unknown like the later 'Maréchal Pétain'. In 1965 he added 'Echard', 'Senegal', and 'Souvenir de Frido fing'.

In 1967 he created display gardens for 'Le Miroir du Parc Floral' at the Floralies in Orleans, fashioning himself Jean Laydeker Propriétaire-Directeur on his business cards. In 1969 the run down Chateau and Park de Vincennes on the eastern reaches of Paris hosted the *Troisièmes Floralies Internationales* which permanently transformed the site. The organisers requested that all exhibitors not only created displays at their own expense but that they also donated all plants used to the Paris authorities. The premise was that the Floralies would provide an excellent international sales forum. Rather bitterly Laydeker noted that the orders placed by visitors did not cover the expense and costs involved, however, he was awarded three prizes: First in the *Concours Technique* [Technical Show], *Prix d'honneur* for *Nymphaea* and First for hardy aquatic plants. He introduced *N.* 'Bateau' the name of the nursery site, and 'Grésille' (probably a reintroduction of 'Grésilias') the name of its small stream. Today the Park provides Paris with 28 hectares of green, floral space in the Bois de Vincennes. There is a strong association with Bagatelle and in 2012 links were re-established between both and Latour-Marliac SARL.

Laydeker handled the nursery's wholesale business efficiently and effectively, in 1972 he named 'Chateau le Rouge' where his grandfather had been born and in his final year, 1974, 'Labeaugere', 'Larroque', and 'Maréchal Petain'. The last has unsurprisingly completely disappeared, presumably renamed. Jean and Marguerite were the last to live in the family house throughout the season where the family would gather annually to celebrate his birthday until his death in 1974.

From the 1950s the nursery was worked by the Maurel family who were living on site. Apart from free accommodation, they received fresh milk and two chickens per week for services rendered. As trade was effectively mail order, the business continued to be operated from Bordeaux by Philippe and Henri Laydeker. In the 1980s their son Guy Maurel worked at the nursery and sold plants direct from the site. Philippe Laydeker would visit weekly during the season. Maurel continued as Manager for the first years after the Davies bought the property in 1991. Maurel now works as groundsman for the Mairie and volunteers with the local fire service whose team members were photographed among the water lilies for their 2012 calendar.

The Latour-Marliac Nursery today and its Gardens

The landscape, before alteration, like the house, was a complex of romantic charm. Water from the spring flowed downward through dense woodlands along the way feeding water shapes made at different dates for different purposes and finally flowing into a partially obscured scene of distant Downs along which ran an ancient way across Southern England. There was never any doubt that it was the thought, presence, act and sound of water that was holding together the competing ideas that had been introduced in the woodlands - ideas remotely associated with Islam, Greece, the Middle Ages, the primeval and other times and cultures. It was not until the summer of 1988, when the view was opened up and an abstract design of a further pool introduced, that a unity of earth and sky became apparent. ... The view only shows the tranquil classical canal leading past observation balconies and water lilies to plunge into twin grottos ...'

Geoffrey Jellicoe on his Garden Design at Shute (1969-1988), published 1991

By 1991 the century-old family connection was fading, the old house was increasingly shut up and the nursery was out of step with the outside world. After Latour-Marliac's death the nursery had evolved into a wholesale, worldwide supplier of water lilies – it is no exaggeration to say that almost every water lily available on the international market before 1970 had its genesis here. At about that time, and exactly one hundred years after the founding of Latour-Marliac's nursery in 1875, across the Pond, a seemingly unrelated birth took place in New Hampshire. Robert, the third child and second son of Richard Sheldon, Professor of Russian Language and Literature at Dartmouth College in

Left: Robina MacIntyre painted this portrait of the thirteen-year-old Robert Sheldon in 1991 from an earlier photograph. This was Sheldon's first lily pond that he created in his parents' garden in New Hampshire. The pink *Nymphaea* 'Marliacea Rosea' remains his favourite.

Above: Cafe Marliacea, the lake and the church spire in Le Temple-sur-Lot. Good food, bamboos, aquatic gardening and a sense of place – the legacy of Latour-Marliac lives on. The roof of the building containing the ancient prune oven can be seen in the top right-hand corner.

Hanover and Karen Sheldon née Sears, was born on 29th December 1975. Karen, an Episcopal priest in the diocese of Vermont, was one of the first women to be ordained in that state. Their doors were open so that their four children were free to go out and explore the natural world that surrounded them, whilst an eclectic mix of people, from academics to exiled Soviet dissidents, were welcomed in through their doors. Thanks to Richard's academic standing, he was regularly invited as a guest speaker on overseas alumni tours, and his young family would accompany him, thereby exploring the wider world.

Early on Robert developed a fascination with reptiles and amphibians. He needed no excuse to plunge into any body of standing water in the quest for frogs, salamanders or, especially, turtles – a spectacle that still takes place on the nursery every year, now for water lily maintenance. When out of the water his interest encompassed all animals, and such was his knack that the local natural history museum would call whenever they found a small orphaned creature. Armed with eye-droppers and enthusiasm he was invariably successful in raising them to independence. One racoon, christened Sweety, became such a permanent fixture that he would sit on the Professor's lap and ransack his pockets.

During the long cold New Hampshire winter of 1987/88 Robert conceived the bright idea of creating a pond to provide a ready-made home for his aquatic finds. The following summer, whilst his parents were away for a couple of days, he decided that this was the perfect moment to start digging. Once they had recovered from the shock, they encouraged him to do a good job. The following winter he discovered the American water gardening industry, scouring catalogues which revealed the joys of specialists such as Lilypons Water Gardens in Maryland and Perry's in North Carolina. The next spring and summer the ugly duckling pond started to evolve into swan status. The Sheldon parents were marshalled into weekend visits to plant nurseries and farmers' markets so that their earnest teenager could cross-examine any specialist who would listen. By the age of sixteen his garden and pond were bringing in similar commissions from his parents' friends and neighbours. After High School he went to McGill University in Montréal where he majored in English Literature. He continued his landscaping business through his first summer vacations but on more mature reflection concluded that the most creative and satisfying aspect of the business, was actually its development rather than the design and building of the gardens. However, he continued to landscape his parents' garden whilst occasionally undertaking pond work for ready money to pay for graduate school.

With his sights set on an entrepreneurial career he moved

to New York to seek his fortune, starting off as a waiter and then becoming a real estate agent on the Upper West Side. Fortunes take many forms and a big sales commission in 2000 freed him to join the dot-com boom. He spent a summer creating one of the first water gardening e-commerce websites, pondforum.com, so honing his skills in selling water lilies and pond equipment. He could tell his 'Marliacea' from his 'Laydekeri' but their original source was as yet unknown to him. Meanwhile back in Le Temple-sur-Lot …

One of the modern references in the archive is a college report written by Henri Laydeker's son Guillaume, born in 1965, which traces the history of the site and its uses from the family point of view. After the family's sale of the company in 1991, he and his father were to become regular visitors, charting the developments that took place under its new management. During Joseph Bory and Édgard Latour-Marliac's tenures, the English were their best customers and now in 1991 they were ready to step in and save this historic nursery.

The Établissements Latour-Marliac was bought from the Laydeker family by the commercially and horticulturally knowledgeable Ray and Barbara Davies in 1991. On what Ray describes as a beautiful day in March, the Davies made their first visit. Looking back he reckons he was most attracted by the quantity of water lilies in the seventy cultivation pools,

which appeared to number in the hundreds of thousands. The trading figures available were not good, but the challenge was exciting and Ray and Barbara were ideal candidates to take it on. At the time the Davies were directors of one of the foremost water garden nurseries in the UK, Stapeley Water Gardens in Nantwich, Cheshire, and it was able to provide the necessary financial stability and staff. They improved Édgard's villa for themselves and their daughter, and added a conservatory as well as converting the 'chalet' around what is believed to be the oldest prune drying oven in France, into a gîte. Both buildings enjoy the historic views across the original *bassins*. A swimming pool was built between and behind the buildings, screened by bamboos. In March 1999, having retired from Stapeley, the Davies purchased a property in

Above: Lotus provide such a magnificent display that it is worth the risk of losing them in a harsh winter. Sheldon firmly advocates that they are hardier than they seem, especially in areas that have hot summers.

Facing page: *Nymphaea* 'Lily Pons', this 'very double' pink was introduced by Perry Slocum in 1993, its parentage might include *N.* 'Gloire du Temple'. The Lilypons Water Gardens in Maryland were an early inspiration for Robert Sheldon.

Cyprus from where they divided their time with the nursery. The Davies were maintaining three National Collections of *Nymphaea*, two in England at Stapeley Water Gardens and at Burnby Hall in Yorkshire, and the one at Latour-Marliac which was overseen by the *Conservatoire des Collections Végétales Spécialisées* (CCVS).

Ray Davies had left school at fifteen to take up an apprenticeship in the Crewe Parks Department in Cheshire, he was appointed Deputy Head Gardener at Reaseheath College, Nantwich. In his spare time he developed a water garden around his mother's house, had a small nursery and undertook landscaping work. In 1965 he left Reaseheath, took out a mortgage and married for the first time. The business thrived and he was joined by his brother Nigel in 1966. In November 1969 they bought a 5.25 acre site at Stapeley which started trading as a Nursery and Water Garden Centre in January 1970, ultimately the site extended to 40 acres. They acted as joint-proprietors of Stapeley Water Gardens until Nigel's untimely death following a swimming accident in America in 1988.

During the 1980s Barbara Dobbins (with Stevie Sheatsley) had created a licensed nursery and landscape contracting business, Santa Barbara Water Gardens and Landscapes (SBWGL) in California. It was the first in the area to offer specialist residential and commercial water garden design, construction, repair and maintenance services. In 1988 Barbara sold out her share of the business to marry Ray, and she became a Director of Stapeley Water Gardens. They were also founding members of the International Water Lily Society (IWLS), for whom Barbara acted as President from 1995 to 1997.

In 1988 the annual IWLS symposium had included both Stapeley and Burnby Hall, three years later the Davies had purchased Établissements Latour-Marliac, which they renamed Établissements Botaniques Latour-Marliac. In 1996 *The Water Garden Journal* ran an article entitled: *La Belle France – The IWLS Pilgrimage to the Cradle of Nymphaea Cultivation* in which it enthused:

'The IWLS Symposium 1996 – France gives participants an opportunity to explore and understand the era and events which inspire Latour-Marliac, the habitats and characteristics of the rarest of his species breeding stock and to acquire an in-depth understanding of the region which produced such a lasting gift to the world of horticulture.

This chance to extensively visit and study at Établissements Botaniques Latour-Marliac, to review original correspondence and documents dating back to 1881 and to gain intimate access to the oldest aquatic plant nursery in the world is truly a once-in-a-lifetime opportunity. Every effort has been made to ensure that multilingual guides will help make every aspect of the visit clear and accessible to all participants. The IWLS Symposium 1996 – France will steal your heart, fill your head, and take your breath away.
Join us!'

Facing page, top: *Nymphaea* 'Barbara Dobbins'. The maiden name of Barbara Davies and named by Kirk Strawn in 1996.

Facing page, bottom: *Victoria* 'Longwood Hybrid'. This hybrid was raised by Patrick Nutt of Longwood Gardens in Pennsylvania who crossed V. cruziana with V. amazonica in the 1960s. As well as the hardy water lilies and lotus pools outside, a glasshouse provides the perfect conditions for tropicals such as Victoria.

Above left: A portrait of Ray Davies amongst the *Victoria* in the glasshouse. Ray and Barbara Davies owned the nursery from 1991 to 2007.

Above right: Barbara Davies. Strawn named two water lilies for Barbara Davies, the first with her married name in 1992, and the second using her maiden name, Barbara Dobbins, in 1996.

Above: Latour-Marliac returned to the Grand Palais for the first time since 1900. In 2013 Robert Sheldon created this exhibit with Interscène, a prominent French landscape architecture firm started by Thierry Huau, for the annual garden event *L'Art du Jardin*.

Facing page: Work undertaken by the Davies in the 1990s.
Top four pictures, clockwise from top left: The Grésille was excavated to create the lake; the steep banks were stablised for planting, note the road bridge from the village at the base; to the left the new glasshouse for tropicals and to the right the embryo mound for the gloriette; view from the mound to the village, later the narrow neck was and still is crossed by a thatched bridge.

Bottom: The large glasshouse (just out of view on the left) built by the Davies is used by Sheldon to display tropicals such as *Victoria* and in 2012 to raise tropical water lilies for exhibitors at the Chelsea Flower Show and in 2013 for *L'Art du Jardin*, above.

The Laydeker family were also invited to unveil Lloyd Le Blanc's bronze statue of Latour-Marliac cradling a *Nymphaea* flower in one hand and a sable paintbrush in the other. After five years of financial and physical investment the Davies could finally enjoy and showcase the fruits of their labours – Latour-Marliac was back on the map. About the same time Barbara obtained the unique distinction of having two modern water lily cultivars named for her, *N.* 'Barbara Dobbins' and *N.* 'Barbara Davies'. Both were bred by their good friend Kirk Strawn who was one of the first to have visited the site in 1991, an experience he would repeat several times. The Davies wanted to build up the tourist potential of the site, which was very run down, so apart from cleaning out the collection ponds and about a fifth of the growing ponds, they undertook extensive landscaping of the adjoining field and orchard. La Grésille, the stream running

through to the Lot, was excavated into a sinuous lake, its spoil landscaped into an undulating *parc* that offers views down and across the site as well as out into the village and countryside. In doing this, some of Latour-Marliac's original, by then very broken, *bassins* were lost. Curiously, although apparently not intended, the new lake spanned at its base with a bridge, creates an immediate association with Monet and his water garden at Giverny. The lake, the bridge and the village beyond create both a sense of place and a connection with the community beyond. In the top corner,

amongst tall bamboos a substantial raised walk is topped by a gazebo which provides a tranquil secluded spot.

Like anyone seeing the thirty-four historic volumes of meticulously handwritten records, the Davies realised the potential for research that lay within. In February 2001 I made my first research visit for *Monet at Giverny* and discussed how a roll call of key gardening personalities graced the pages. The Davies also saw the need for a standard work on water lily identification and correct nomenclature. To that end, Ray collaborated with a small

team to record all known varieties with full descriptions and illustrated with high quality botanical watercolours. Extensive research was carried out during the 1990s and subsequently the *Water Lily Monograph* was published in April 2004.

Once installed at Le Temple-sur-Lot, the Davies soon discovered that the wholesale market was dire and unprofitable. In tandem with improving the site, they developed the idea of retailing containerised water lilies in three-litre pots (and larger) without holes. As a result, and in the absence of a significant mail order business, very few were sold bare-rooted directly from Latour-Marliac's original *bassins*. They introduced five new water lilies. The first 'Julien Decelle', in 1991, is open to debate as it may well be a re-introduction, then in 1992 'Jean Laydeker' which was a renaming of 'Guy Maurel' and has now reverted to the original. Finally in 1993 'Pam Bennett' and 'Temple Fire' made their debut. However, the archives reveal unpleasant difficulties with staff, poor visitor numbers and cultural clashes, all of which undermined their achievements.

In 2003 Robert Sheldon moved to France to do his doctorate, by chance he found the nursery on the web and, like so many, was thrilled by the Monet connection. In the summer of 2004 he made a pilgrimage to the site and met Barbara. Keen to do more than pondforum.com, Robert offered to redesign their embryo website and manage their online sales. However, the proposal went no further as Barbara and Ray had decided to divorce. Robert returned to his doctorate and phased out his e-commerce website whilst

Barbara ran the Établissements Botaniques Latour-Marliac alone. Nearly two years later, as Robert was preparing to teach a graduate marketing course at the Sorbonne in Paris, he needed to give the students an end of term project. Their assignment was to write a European-scale marketing plan for a real firm, and what could be more interesting than one for Établissements Botaniques Latour-Marliac. However, when Robert called for catalogues he discovered that the telephone line had been disconnected. After a few days he satisfied his lingering curiosity by ringing the Mairie in Le Temple-sur-Lot only to learn that the company was in liquidation and they were looking for a *repreneur*. A few days elapsed before he called to ask for the number of the liquidator and so the process towards acquisition started.

Facing page: With the aid of artificial light and heat Sheldon has been experimenting with raising *Victoria* on site from seed in the glasshouse.

Above: The new *parc* is approached across the lake by the Monet bridge at the far end or, as seen here, over a thatched bridge. This was recovered in 2011 as part of ongoing extensive restoration. The glasshouse can be seen in the background.

Overleaf: A capricchio of water lilies, nursery, village and large glasshouse. Buoyant colourful water lilies nestle amongst reflections of sky and clouds. To the left the extensive greenhouse raised by the Davies. The church steeple is embosomed by the mature trees on the site.

Silas Berkowitz, one of the interns for the summer of 201 , lifting and dividing roots of *Nymphaea* 'Comanche' for mail order.

The original Latour-Marliac methods of only using the cultivation ponds has been resumed. Here a root of *Nymphaea* 'Colonel Welch' is being harvested for sale. If properly monitored this traditional method ensures that the water lilies do not become choked but grow freely whilst routine weeding and maintenance can be carried out at the same time.

The terracotta dishes that line the *bassins* are too fragile for everyday use, so plastic pans are used to hold water lilies whilst routine maintenance or harvesting are taking place.

All aquatic plants being sent by mail order are thoroughly cleaned before packing.

Lotus ready for despatch.

Tropical water lilies ready for despatch.

Stocks of tropical water lilies are air freighted into Bordeaux airport, Sheldon collects them and then raises them in the glasshouse. This consignment arrived in March for growing on, ready to be used at the Chelsea Flower Show.

One of the other uses for the *bassins* is to root new plants such as these lotus, seen here weighted down by a stone whilst they establish themselves.

The nursery closes in October and the task of emptying and repairing the *bassins* starts

Robert Sheldon shovels out the build-up of muck along the bottom of the *bassin*.

A wheelbarrow has been converted to move the pump from *bassin* to *bassin*.

The water lilies are lifted to be split, weeded and repotted ready to be put back in the clean *bassins*.

Left: Small water lily plants are stored in plastic pans whilst the maintenance is undertaken.

Below: The traditional art nouveau *bassins* are emptied every year in October for maintenance.

Splitting water lily plants before placing them in one of the pans.

A range of pans and dishes line the *bassins*, they will be used for water lilies awaiting splitting, moving and general attention.

Cleaning and repairing any leaks as well as ensuring a waterproof surface is a dusty, backbreaking job.

Once all the maintenance has been undertaken the pools are refilled and the water lilies replanted.

Happily resettled the leaves of a water lily make their way to the surface.

Robert Sheldon believes that a very high level of maintenance is key to ensuring that customers and tourists leave satisfied.

As the contract would not be finalised until September 2007, Sheldon decided that he had no choice but to start work with just a verbal agreement. He reckoned that trust was a better option than six months further neglect. Ray met him on site and handed over the keys – Sheldon knew how

to grow aquatic plants, build and maintain ponds and indeed how to sell water lilies. These skills and his education (an advanced degree in the humanities and in business, including a PhD in Organisation Science from Sciences Po, one of France's most prestigious schools) enabled him to review the nursery with an eye to its economic future as well as retaining a poetic empathy with its history. He is also bilingual. However, as he had never been a nurseryman, he faced a vertiginous learning curve. By the time he took over in 2007 there was no wholesale business, just a small retail mail order business and some on site sales. The infrastructure was intact but the once new *parc* had become overgrown and everything needed rewiring, painting and generally redoing. Overall Latour-Marliac's original seventy *bassins* were in a pretty parlous state, many choked with organic material and infested with the dreaded crayfish. The acidic water, predators and more vigorous water lilies had destroyed several varieties. Furthermore, there were no individual labels, identification of the *Nymphaea* was based

Facing page: The Davies started the renovation of the culture and exhibition ponds which Sheldon has almost completed. Cleaned and renewed they provide perfect frames such as can be seen here with *Nymphaea* 'Starbright'.

Below: The lake is graced by swans, however, the scene is misleadingly tranquil, in 2011 a *silure* (like a very large catfish) ate all the cygnets, local gossip and media warned that it was three metres long. A public warning was issued on the dangers of leaving babies near the banks of the River Lot in case they were snapped up by this beast. A *Jaws* experience that is rather at odds with the delicate associations of water nymphs.

on a book listing, in some instances rather approximately, what was in each *bassin*.

Sheldon made it his goal to redo every one of the 70 *bassins* on site, a monumental task that was 90 per cent complete, five years after his acquisition of the site. Sheldon is taking the nursery forward by imbibing the best of the traditional Latour-Marliac methods whilst making full use of modern network and marketing opportunities. For example, the world has access to the Latour-Marliac website, which gives a comprehensive guide to the availability, price, appearance and practicalities of *Nymphaea* and aquatic

plants in French and English. The unique Art Nouveau *bassins*, supplemented by the more utilitarian rectangular pools created by the Laydeker descendents, have not only historic interest but Sheldon is firmly convinced that they also remain the best way of raising water lilies for sale. What is more, the nursery can provide one-to-one customer care, offering quality, expertise and fulfilling individual needs. Every year the overall setting is noticeably enhanced, not least during my research visits from 2010 to 2014, so that visitors come to look, relax, stroll and refresh themselves, whether they garden or not. The *bassins* are populated by amphibians whose life cycle can be observed from tiny myriad tadpoles darting under the leaves, developing into ever larger toads and frogs that leap in and out on hot summer days. Beginning in March and ending in July, the soundscape of the nursery is dominated by the croaks, trills and crescendos of at least five different frog species. Eerily the cacophany stops instantly the moment someone passes by.

Gardeners looking for inspiration and to establish what might be feasible in their garden, can take an informative virtual visit in the boutique and then step out to see every imaginable aquatic plant growing *in situ* across over 2.5 hectares of ponds and gardens. Plants are selected and harvested on the spot from their designated *bassins* for both mail order and on-site customers.

Facing page, top: The Davies positioned the gloriette or gazebo on the highest part of the *parc* from which visitors can enjoy excellent views down over the lake. Sheldon has created sweeping blocks of herbaceous perennials interspersed with shrubs.

Facing page, bottom: A summer view from the 'Monet' bridge back across the lake with the ground behind leading up to the gazebo.

Above: Not water lilies, but a Monet moment as visitors to the nursery can sit and enjoy a ringside seat under the arbour resplendent with wisteria to quietly observe the water lilies.

Above: *Nymphaea* 'Colorado' is a Strawn cross that was introduced in 1994.

Left: *Nymphaea* 'Rose Magnolia' in one of the ponds at the Latour-Marliac nursery. 'But by far the most beautiful tribe of Aquatic plants is the Water Lilies – those lovely Naiads that adorn the lakes and rivers with their ample foliage, in tropical as well as temperate lands and, raising their gorgeous flowers with the morning sun, recline them 'In graceful attitudes, to rest', as the god of day sinks in the western horizon.' Henry Lawson (1867-1922).

Whether buying or viewing, the *bassins* display the Latour-Marliac and Laydeker hybrids as well as bringing new hybrids to market from around the world. Attention is paid to ensure that a balance is maintained in the cultivation pools. A successful system means that the plants are kept vigorous by weeding and dividing at the moment of harvest. This is Latour-Marliac's traditional regime, and following it means that the customer is virtually guaranteed vigorous and healthy plants.

Like his predecessors Sheldon is based in two places. In the autumn and winter he is in Paris, where he is a professor and researcher of innovation and entrepreneurship at a business school, and during the spring and summer he is in Le Temple. The company today employs more people than

perhaps at any time in its history, but the numbers remain relatively small. In addition to Sheldon, who visitors may find alternately digging plants for them, serving as cashier, weeding or waiting on tables, the permanent staff consists of a General Manager, a Production Manager and a Head Gardener. During the peak season a full-time worker is employed to work in production. The downstairs rooms of the chalet gîte and Édgard's villa were converted to professional kitchen spaces in 2009. These are used to service the restaurant's terraces, seating seventy-five, which are located adjacent to Latour-Marliac's original Art Nouveau *bassins* and overlook the lake. In addition to local wines and regional specialities such as foie gras, the menu also includes, incidentally, a Godefroy-Lebeuf burger.

The restaurant activity requires a service manager and cook from Easter to September, plus one or two full-time assistants. To this team are added the summer interns, which Sheldon attracts using the lure of the nursery's history and its location. He casts his net wide, advertising annually at European and North American universities for students with a working

---

Facing page: Ancient Egyptians are depicted in pavilions gazing over pools of blue water lilies, today photographers wonder whether they can adequately catch the moment.

Below: Robert Sheldon and General Manager, Charlotte Rousseau.

knowledge of French – unsurprisingly he has always had many more applications than he can accept. They are paid a modest wage for the full range of nursery and café tasks required with free accommodation in the upstairs of Édgard's villa on the nursery. This has proved a successful formula for all involved, and amazingly the interns also manage to find some nightlife.

The small *parc* with the lake at its centre has been further improved with the addition of ever more perennial beds, and it is planned to hold weddings here. In the future guests at such events will arrive through this gardened landscape, their eyes drawn up to the gazebo from which the view down along the elevated walk back to the lake and across to the *bassins* provides an alluring first impression. The atmosphere

within its boundaries and the wider historic, rural setting all add to its beauty. Currently one arrives next to a vast bamboo border that is 30 feet high and runs along the flattest part of the site past the loading bay and the boutique. This entry makes it difficult to appreciate the sinuous shapes of the ponds, the reflective qualities of the water and just the sense of place. However, once you step into the boutique the first impression is good – intelligent displays, excellent books and good products. Currently there is no further in-house breeding work but Sheldon maintains a wide scientific network and is open to innovative botanical research. There is an excellent and burgeoning mail-order service and a strong association with a new retail outlet in Giverny. I have had pleasure in renewing links between Latour-Marliac and Gravetye Manor as well as furthering the association with the *Fondation Monet* at Giverny.

Above: The boutique glimpsed to the left through the blossoms of *Aponogeton* 'Aponogeton distachyos'. The flowers are deliciously fragrant raw in salads.

Left: Latour-Marliac took a healthy interest in local products, not least wines from the Bordeaux region. Sheldon makes his own selection which are then suitably labelled and served in the café.

Facing page: Whether you want to grow water lilies or not the pools, lake and peace of the site have created a tranquil environment where people like to come just to watch (and eat and drink).

The site is also a haven and breeding ground for wildlife such as red squirrels whose kittens gambol around the nursery in the spring, and large noisy hedgehogs. The lake is part of a water system that leads into the canal through the village, which in turn flows to the River Lot. When the lake was created no-one took into account the amount of sediment and debris that naturally accumulates there, so in the long term, unless radical action is taken, it will completely silt up. The groups of water lilies that colonise the limpid lake surface belie the deleterious actions of Enemy Number One, coypu. Given the opportunity, the river rat can wreak untold damage to both the banks and the roots of aquatic plants. Despite this localised havoc, not forgetting the ebb and flow of the century after Latour-Marliac's death, his horticultural venture continues to flourish in ways he could not have imagined.

Although the Lot-et-Garonne does not have the buzz of the Dordogne or Bordeaux, the tourism activity that was started by the Davies and developed by Sheldon has become a major part of the business. Latour-Marliac is nearly the third most visited historical tourist attraction in the Lot-et-Garonne, which in turn provides opportunities for the otherwise sleepy hamlet of Le Temple-sur-Lot. Achieving this has required a concerted approach, including the creation of a popular restaurant, but fundamentally it has been getting the ponds into good shape, and so supporting healthy populations of water lilies and lotus. Buying customers find almost unrivalled choice with over 250 varieties for sale, from the oldest and rarest to the newest and most exotic. In the midst of such a picturesque and historical setting, tourists and local visitors alike can speculate on whether there is anywhere on Earth where one might see water lilies in such numbers and varieties. As Sheldon says: 'People come to Latour-Marliac to see and be among these spectacular plants. They are the raison d'être of all the businesses, be it mail order plant sales, our restaurant or the boutique'. So the invitation offered by Latour-Marliac to William Robinson on 18th May 1896 is still valid but now open to all: 'You must also take account of the most favourable hours in which to see them fully open, these are from 11am until 3pm. In consequence it will be absolutely essential that I lead you around my pools during these timings so we must organise our meal times in the most advantageous manner for viewing the flowers.' And what's more, today visitors can feast in every sense from the comforts of a ringside seat.

The Latour-Marliac Guide to Growing Hardy Water Lilies

Among the most ancient of plants, water lilies have changed little from the Early Cretaceous period, 125 million years ago. They grow from rhizomes, much like iris, but unlike iris they are rooted in the bottom of shallow ponds, lakes and slow-moving rivers. Hardy water lilies will grow anywhere in Europe and will survive winters even in northern Canada.

Choosing the right variety

Beyond aesthetics, the other important criterion to consider when choosing a water lily variety is the depth of the pond. The planting depth is the distance between the mud in which the lily is planted, be it in a pot or on the pond bottom and the surface. They classify these water lilies into three size categories that correspond to depth. Large lilies should be planted at a depth of 40cm to 100cm; medium lilies at a depth of 20cm to 60cm, and small lilies at a depth of 20cm to 40cm. Lilies classified as very small or very large may be planted in as little as 10cm or as much as 1.5m of water respectively. If your pond is very deep, or too deep for a small or medium lily, you can easily raise the level of the planting container using bricks or cinderblocks.

Planting Water Lilies

In Europe, hardy water lilies may be planted from March through to November and they will flower on and off from May to October.

Choose the right spot. Water lilies need full sun. A minimum of 6 to 7 hours a day of sun will ensure that your lilies flower to their full potential. Don't forget to take into account the surrounding vegetation so that colours and bloom times are complementary.

Choose the ideal planting container and earth. At Latour-Marliac they use 14 L round planting containers with no holes. There is nothing wrong with using the perforated "aquatic planting" containers found in garden centres, but they offer no special advantages to the plants and they make division difficult (and they usually break during division). Their pots are 14L as they hold about as much material as one person can safely manipulate. The ideal soil to use is a simple clay-rich topsoil. Avoid compost and other light planting mixtures.

   The rhizome should be planted more or less horizontally, so that the stems are at a 90-degree angle with the soil. The crown of the rhizome, the point where the leaves and stems protrude, should remain at or near the surface of the soil. Make sure to water down the pot before submerging it to eliminate air bubbles. Insert three fertiliser tablets a finger-length into the soil in a triangle around the rhizome.

Caring for Water Lilies

In order to maintain your water lilies you will need to fertilise them once a year (if they are planted in containers) and divide them every three years. Neglect in either of these areas can lead to diminution of leaf size and a lack of flowers and in the worst case the death of the water lily from overcrowding.

Fertilising. Latour-Marliac recommend using a chemical fertiliser in tablet form. The tablet form allows you to insert the fertiliser into the soil, where it will not diffuse into the pond water. They use a nitrogen-rich formula of Osmocote in tablet form. These have the advantage of being slow-release (application once per year), whereas the tablets marketed as specifically for aquatic plants need to be reapplied every four to eight weeks. Certain Marliac varieties such as 'Seignoureti', 'Indiana' or similar respond best to organic fertilisers, certainly bone and blood meal.

Dividing. Every three or four years you will need to remove the lilies from their planting container and divide them so that they don't choke each other out. Dividing lilies requires some work but it's not complicated. Isolate and remove the rhizomes. Keep any healthy rhizome that has a crown pushing leaves and buds. Cut away excess rhizome, leaving 6-8cm of rhizome behind the crown. Replant these in fresh soil. The best time to divide is in April or September, but it can be done at almost any time.

Water lily Troubleshooting

Fungus based diseases

Brown or red spots on the pads usually indicate the presence of Ramularia nymphaerum. This fungus requires acidic water to prosper, therefore the best treatment option is to add ilme to the water to bring up the Ph, ideally dolomitic lime. The recommended dosage is 3 cups of lime per cubic metre of water, added around the affected plants.This disease is not fatal, but it should be treated as it is unsightly and can act as a gateway for more serious problems.

Crown rot, caused by phytopthora, is the most serious disease to afflict a water lily. Symptoms include a uniform and premature yellowing of the leaves, which then detach from the rhizome. On close inspection, the rhizome will smell like sour milk. If the disease is not treated, the principal rhizome will die. Phytopthora requires acidic conditions to proliferate, so initial treatment should involve heavy doses of dolomotic lime in the water column surrounding the affected plants, around 5 cups per cubic metre. Failing that, powerful antifungal product exists that will clear phytopthora while reinforcing the plant's immune system to prevent subsequent infections. Manufacturer instructions should be followed closely.

Insects

The black water lily aphid (Rhopalosiphum nymphaeae) can be a nuisance beginning in early summer and it will attack other aquatic plants as well. Aphids pierce the leaves and stems of plants in order to eat the sap. If left untreated they will cause leaves to yellow and can render the lily vulnerable to other infections. Aphids can be drowned by dousing the lilies with the garden hose, or by spritzing them with any viscous mixture such as water and liquid soap. There are also a number of effective treatments available at your local garden centre. The China mark moth (Clophila nymphaeata) is easily recognisable because the caterpillars will cut out pieces of the pad in order to make their cocoons. The water lily leaf beetle (Galerucella nymphaeae) is 5mm in size and black in colour. It carves unsightly trails over lily pads. Both the China mark and the leaf beetle can be effectively treated with products containing Bacillus thuringiensis. The bacteria disrupt the insects' digestive systems causing death within a few days. It is sold at most garden centres under various brand names.

Other pests include coypu (Myocastor coypus), which are aquatic rat-like creatures the size of small dogs. Coypu were introduced to Europe from South America and they need to eat 25 per cent of their body weight per day in aquatic plants in order to survive. They pose a problem mainly for those with natural ponds and waterways. Crayfish can also harm water lilies, as can turtles and certain type of plant-eating carp.

Below: Nymphaea 'Princess Elizabeth'. Introduced by Jean Laydeker in 1939, after he had received permission from King George V to name a water lily after his daughter. The lily is easy to grow and look after and has a delicate perfume.

Acknowledgements

First and foremost I want to thank Robert Sheldon for his unfailing generosity during the many weeks I spent at Le Temple-sur-Lot and in Paris. Researching the archives and watching the water lilies grow through every season has given a whole new meaning to primary sources. Rob also engineered multiple introductions, fed me very well and pours a mean gin and tonic. So what more can I say? My quest to undertake this work was fired during my first stay with Ray and Barbara Davies, also generous hosts. For this book Ray provided further very useful information and encouragement. Charlotte Rousseau, Latour-Marliac's General Manager, helped in many ways not least being unfailingly warm, enthusiastic and efficient. In summer 2011 Silas Berkowitz, an intern on the nursery, donated his spare time to typing up some of the key letters in the archives, no mean task for a generation not accustomed to deciphering hand writing especially in a foreign language.

Amongst the many libraries I visited, I especially want to acknowledge the ever helpful and encouraging Elizabeth Koper at the RHS Lindley Library. I am delighted to report that growing water lilies goes hand in hand with enjoying good food for which I thank Charlotte de Rothschild at Exbury, James Priest at Giverny, and Tom Coward at Gravetye Manor.

The original book was commissioned to run to a maximum of 50,000 words, such were the my so fascinating details I unearthed, my final copy totaled 71,000 words. Angela Linforth deserves awards in diplomacy and literary juggling for her skilled nipping and tucking when editing my passionate outpourings. Far from lost, many of the detailed trimmings will be gracing my talks and lectures. My gratitude to Lynn Taylor for coming up trumps with the final design. Also Melanie Aspey at the Rothschild Archives. Finally thanks to Pete Evans for adding his artistry to viewing water lilies.

Bibliography

Bradley-Hole, Kathryn	*Lost Gardens of England from the archives of Country Life*, Aurum Press, 2004
Colquhoun, Kate	*A Thing in Disguise – The Visionary Life of Joseph Paxton*, Harper Perennial, 2004
Conard, Henry	*The waterlilies: a monograph of the genus* Nymphaea *with an introduction by Philip Swindells* (Facsimile 1905 edition), 1991
Forge, Andrew	*Monet – Art Institute of Chicago* (Artists in Focus), 1995
Goodyear, W.H.	*The Grammar of the Lotus*, 1981
Grey, R.M.	*New Hybrid Nymphaeas in American Gardening*
Holmes, Caroline	*Impressionists in their Gardens*, Garden Art Press, 2012
Holmes, Caroline	*Monet at Giverny*, Garden Art Press, 2013
Lauzan, Philippe	*Correspondance de Bory de Saint-Vincent*, 1908
Leyel, Mrs. C.F.	*Compassionate Herbs*, Faber & Faber, 1946
Leyel, Mrs. C.F.	*Elixirs of Life*, Faber & Faber, 1948
Miller, Naomi	*Heavenly Caves Reflections on the Garden Grotto*, George Brazilier, 1982
Ottewill, David	*The Edwardian Garden*, Yale University Press, 1989
Russell, Vivien	*Monet's Water Lilies*, Frances Lincoln, 1998
Shephard, Sue	*Seeds of Fortune – A Gardening Dynasty*, Bloomsbury, 2003

Useful Websites:

Holmes, Caroline	www.caroline-holmes.com
Latour-Marliac SARL	www.latour-marliac.com
Leblanc, Lloyd, sculptor	www.leblancfineart.com

Picture Credits

All photography by Peter Evans (www.painting-photography-france.com; www.peter-evans-photographer.com) unless stated otherwise.

Latour-Marliac SARL
Title page, Prelim, Pages 9, 11, 15 upper, 17 upper, lower, 18/19, 20-21, 29, 31, 32, 33, 35, 36, 37 lower, 38 upper, middle, 39, 43 upper, lower, 44, 45, 53 lower, 54, 56, 57, 58/59, 60, 67, 68 upper, 69, 70 left middle, lower, right, 71 lower left, 72, 73, 77, 78, 79 upper, lower, 80, 84/85, 86 upper, lower, 87, 88, 91, 93, 94/95, 96 upper, lower, 97, 98 upper, lower, 102, 103 upper, lower, 104, 105 upper, lower, 107, 108 upper, 109, 110 upper, 111, 114, 116 lower, 117, 118/119, 120 upper, lower, 122/123, 124 lower, 127 lower, 129 upper, lower, 136, 138 lower, 144/145, 147, 148 lower left, 152, 153, 158, 159, 162, 163 lower, 164 upper, 165 upper, 166/167, 169 upper, lower, 170, 173 upper, 174 lower, 176, 177, 180 upper, 181, 182 upper, lower, 183, 194 upper, 195, 198, 200, 203

Caroline Holmes
Frontispiece, Pages 6-7, 15 lower, 16 upper, lower, 23, 25, 27, 37 upper, 38 lower, 42, 49, 53 top right, 55 upper, 61, 62, 63 upper, 65, 66 lower, 68 lower, 70 upper, 71 upper, 90, 98 lower, 115 upper, lower, 116 upper, 126 lower, 130/131, 132, 134, 140, 148 upper, 149 upper, lower, 154 upper, lower, 156, 157, 165 lower, 172, 174 upper, 175, 184, 185, 188 all, 189 all, 190 all, 191 all

Public Domain 28, 50, 52, 54, 63 (lower), 151; **Archives départementales de l'Eure** 135; **Bridgeman,** 141, 142; **Rex Features** 143; **Panteek.com** 151; **Rothschild Archives** 163

One of Peter Evans' photography students at Latour-Marliac.

Index

Page numbers in **bold** refer to images

Plant Index
Page numbers in **bold** refer to images

Claude Monet Giverny 17 avril

14 courant

8, 60ᵉ

B. Latour Marliac

17 avril par un colis postal en gare Vernon

Monsieur le Gérant de
l'Intendance de son Al-
tesse Royale le Prince de
Bulgarie — Sophia,

Nous avons pris bonne note
vot ordre du 3 courant
e vous expédier quelques
emplaires des plantes suivantes
t avez formé la liste.
Nymphaea Seignouret

— Marliacea

— flammea

— ignea

— rubra punctata

Mᵣ J. Leemann
Heaton Mersey.

Cher Monsieur,

Selon votre désir je vo
expédié, hier, par colis po
fleurs, du magnifique N
aquarrea; du N. La
e sens, du N. Arc-en-

---

6 Janvier 12

Monsieur le Directeur
du Journal "The Garde
Londres.

Cher Monsieur,
Comme l'a
derniè, Je vous prie de f
insérer l'annonce ci-jointe
six numéros consécutifs
Journal "The Garden
partir du prochain nu
Dès que cette in

Monsieur Jas Hudson
Gunnersbury House
Cher Monsieur,
Quand j'ai eu
le plaisir de vous voir au
temple je vous avais
promis deux choses:
1° de vous envoyer la
photographie de mon
pauvre père au